NEW SOCIOLOGY LIBRARY

No. 4

General Editor : Professor NORBERT ELIAS
Department of Sociology, University of Leicester

Sociology of Literature

Sociology of Literature

By

Robert Escarpit

Translated by Ernest Pick

SECOND EDITION

With a new introduction by

Professor MALCOLM BRADBURY
School of English and American Studies,
University of East Anglia

and Dr. BRYAN WILSON
All Souls College, Oxford

FRANK CASS & CO. LTD.
1971

Published by
FRANK CASS AND COMPANY LIMITED
67 Great Russell Street, London WC1B 3BT
by arrangement with Presses Universitaires de France

New introduction Copyright © 1971 M. Bradbury and B. Wilson

First French edition   1958
First English edition   1965
Second English edition   1971

ISBN 0 7146 2729 1

Printed in Great Britain by
Biddles Ltd., Guildford, Surrey

INTRODUCTION

I

Robert Escarpit's *Sociology of Literature* first appeared in France in 1958 and was an early statement in a line of enquiry that has become more and more important over the last fifteen years. There are various reasons why, in our time, two disciplines that have thought of themselves as distinct and separate—literary study and sociology—should attempt to explore common ground. One obvious reason is the growing predominance of sociology in *all* our thinking. Sociology has been the remarkable growth-subject of the postwar years; and the apparent scale of its pretensions, its seeming capability to account for a large number of social and human manifestations, has proved remarkably attractive to those seeking new intellectual syntheses. In a time of increasing relativism and increasing social change, it appears to offer, if not solutions, then at least 'objective' and ranging perceptions which let us see old experience with new eyes. It has been not only the great synthetic discipline of the postwar period; it has also been in certain respects the discipline which has most fully echoed and perhaps promoted the growing disenchantment of men in a democratic-egalitarian society with the rules, traditions and modus operandi of society in the past. It has been a discipline which has encouraged us to see that things apparently magisterial and eternal (like literature itself) are products of social funding and subject to social change. It has helped to support the growing feeling that the valid expressive culture of a society lies not simply in its magisterial works, but in less elevated, less art-conscious forms as well. It has encouraged concern with the general expression of creativity within society of which the serious literature can be seen as but one form. In short, interest in a sociological approach to literature has been part of a growing interest in the broad cultural stock of society at all its levels—an interest, of course, by no means new in literary criticism or intellectual discussion of the arts, but one which sociology can expand. But literary study and sociology are both distinct disciplines with strikingly different premises and methods, and the development of an effective debate in the field of literature-and-sociology was inevitably slow. Interesting works in the area have been produced; but there are certain reasons why difficulty is bound to occur. One of these reasons is understandable methodological suspicion on the part of many literary critics—or perhaps rather a note of puzzled enquiry: in what way do perceptions derived from considering literature as a social manifestation aid in their two main activities of elucidation and evaluation? The other is the relatively small place given to literary and cultural experience in most of the models of society which have been produced by modern sociologists. Many of them have regarded the arts and culture generally as an entirely derivative part of the superstructure of society. Despite a growing awareness among sociologists that in post-industrial society leisure becomes a significant area of social concern, nevertheless the increasingly scientistic approach of the discipline and its somewhat superior attitude toward humane studies has left the field of the sociology of literature a rather neglected area, thought to be of only marginal importance. Fortunately there are signs that at least a few contemporary sociologists do not see their discipline as inevitably opposed to cultural values as such (even though they still endorse a generally value-neutral attitude to their own work) and the sociology of literature now enjoys some slightly greater acceptibility.[1]

From these two directions, then, the challenge to the traditional approach to literature—to what Robert Escarpit calls the "classical framework of the man and his work" within which literature is usually seen and discussed—has developed, and has developed quite variously. Robert Escarpit calls his book *Sociology of Literature*. The title is encouraging, even though we can now see that it is too grand. There are now several sociologies of literature, of which M. Escarpit's kind is one—though an early and a very thorough-going one. In England we have seen the development of another, that kind of culture-and-society approach which grows out of the preoccupation of a long line of English writers and critics with the overall state of cultural affairs and with the quality of life in society generally. The modern carriers of this tradition are critics like Richard Hoggart and Raymond Williams, who have produced remarkable work from a much more positively literary approach than that of Escarpit, and who have added new dimensions to the field. There has also been an important contribution from a neo-sociological approach which has been concerned, much more than M. Escarpit is, with the *content* of literature, its nature, its structure, its artistic complexity. That these things can be seen profitably as in some sense social derivatives has been made clear in books like Leo Lowenthal's *Literature and the Image of Man*, which, written by a sociologist, proposes that "All literary materials, including those hitherto considered beyond the province of the sociologist, . . . assume social meanings", and that "the writer not only reports how the individual reacts to the pressures of society; he also offers a picture of changing views about the comparative importance of psychic and social forces". But there is a third kind of approach, one that is notable for its lack of direct contentiousness, since it runs no obvious risk of destroying the internal validity of works of art by distorting or misreading them, namely that of the study of the entire environment of literary creation, distribution and consumption. This area, the exploration not of literature's content but of its context, is the main field of Robert Escarpit's attention in *Sociology of Literature*.

As the author points out, however, this is not simply a matter of acquiring subsidiary data which enlarges our knowledge of the background while telling us very little about the nature or texture of literature itself. His opening pages indicate that his book is an attempt to work on one area while suggesting the larger possibilities of a sociological approach to literature; and that is basic to its importance. One of the demands of the book is that we consider just what it is we mean when we attribute to a particular book the quality of being 'literature'. For 'literature' is not the constant we sometimes think it to be. Literature does not have a fixed status; it is part of the larger total world of the book, which includes many forms of expression of which literature is one. Particular books may be regarded as 'literature' at some times but not at others; they may be used by readers as literature or as something else. To understand what literature is, Escarpit tells us, we need to explore the "specificity of the literary fact": we need to explore the character of the three basic elements he sees as determining the social existence of 'literature'; that "circuit of inter-relationship" that binds writer, book, and reader into a complex—a complex which involves problems of a psychological, moral, æsthetic, political and economic kind at all points in the circuit. For while one of the essential values embodied in literature is that it is capable of representing and dramatising individuality and independence of mind and spirit, of manifesting an ideal of free expression; and while the ideal portrait of the creative process is of an act pursued in freedom, solitude and without constraint, the fact remains that by another definition the writer is neither solitary nor autonomous. He is bound into his time, and lives within its horizons and potentials for thought and vision. He is also bound into a body of practices, conventions, and precepts—bound by the language he uses, which is never alone personal; by the orders and structures with which he shapes and designs his material; and by much more practical conventions of his profession and his craft, such as those which tell him what a novel, a poem, or a play is, as an exchangable or shareable object. Then again there are the simple practical conditions of communication itself; the writer, once he offers to publish, enters a work of publishers and printers, bookshops and booksellers, purchasers and borrowers. Somehow he must be financed; and, if he is to preserve the autonomy and the time to pursue and explore the creative act in a continuous and creative way, he must find a continuous pattern of finance. If his work is to endure, then it must endure physically—by being reprinted by publishers, or by being stored in places of public concourse called libraries. And to complete the circuit there must be comprehending conspirators called readers, who acquire, use, and value books for a complex of purposes and maintain the climate of interest and selectivity out of which the very notion of 'literature' is possible. Other agents are involved: critics and interpreters, reviewers and, increasingly, teachers who transmit both a canon of selection and the means or tactics by which selection may be practised, value or pleasure gained, the circuit completed. Part at least of the development of literature is derived from such very specific matters, from changes in the way writers find their careers, relate to readers, make their income, acquire their reputations, live their lives. An obvious part of a writer's nature lies in his way of being an explorer of the particular possibilities and limitations of the culture in which he acts. He has to make the best of the conditions of expression as they appear to him; he may himself go out to try to alter them, by reaching to new audiences or new methods of selling, by finding new tones and nuances that bind him to a novel community which is his particular audience. Many of the changing factors in literary expression are highly specific ones; writers find and make their own continuous identities out of their own origins and the dispositions they see in their audiences. Indeed writers are in part the creation of these dispositions.

Clearly to comprehend this is to reach only to the beginning of a response to literature, and Robert Escarpit's approach to the "specificity of the literary fact" is largely a documentary approach. A literary critic might want to point out that the apparent neutrality of his tone—almost the *irony* of his tone—is built on a recognizable paradox. The paradox is that literature is a centre of values, but sociology seeks to treat values as facts, and to be value-free. We *know* that art is more than the metaphor by which he interprets it, the metaphor of business and technology. "Each and every literary fact presupposes a writer, a book and reader; or, in general terms, an author, a product and a public. By way of an extremely complex transmitting mechanism, a circuit of interrelationships is constituted.

It combines art, technology and business, uniting well-defined individuals in a more or less anonymous though limited community," he tells us at the beginning of the book. We would probably most of us feel that the emphasis determines his discoveries; and that given this language there will be little to say for art.* But the basic presumption—that literature is, *amongst other things*, "the production segment of the book industry, as reading is its consumption segment"—does produce its genuine illuminations. The reader who wants to make his way toward literature from this situation would do well to read, say, Q. D. Leavis's *Fiction and the Reading Public*, that early classic in the field published back in 1932; F. R. Leavis's attack on L. Schucking's *The Sociology of Literary Taste*; and Ian Watt's *The Rise of the Novel* (1947) to see how insights like this can be used—but also be qualified *in* being used—for literary judgment.[2] Nonetheless, Robert Escarpit's book is an important statement, interesting for its specific detail and for its methodology. He extends in this book the possibilities of a sociology of literature, and he does so by concentrating on questions which have not been widely or well explored (except, as he says, by the book-trade itself and by librarians as an instrument of planning). His brief book raises many different lines of particular enquiry, some of them touched on by others and some hardly touched at all.

From the point of view of the English reader, two difficulties with M. Escarpit's book may be encountered. The first is the stress, in his historical account of the sociology of literature, on the 'European' approach; he neglects to mention the importance that cultural criticism of a somewhat different kind has had in the English tradition. The best account of that is to be found in Raymond Williams's *Culture and Society* (1958), and the reader might reflect on the marked procedural differences between the 'English' and the 'European' approach. The distinction being made here has been elaborated at greater length by one of the present authors elsewhere;[3] here it may be briefly said that the European approach has been a good deal more concerned with literature as a phenomenon, an event in society shaped by that society, rather than as a creative force operative in society, which has been what has been commonly assumed in the English cultural debate. M. Escarpit's brief summary of the approach can be extended by reference to Jacques Leenhardt, "The Sociology of Literature: Some Stages in Its History", in *The International Social Science Journal*, XIX, 4 (1967); and the essay by Lucien Goldmann in the same volume

---

* Similar problems arise in sociological discussion of religion, where the ethical neutrality tends to produce linguistic systems that deflate, albeit unconsciously, the subject studied.

called "The Sociology of Literature: Status and Problems of Method" takes the discussion further. The second difficulty lies in the fact that, although M. Escarpit does refer comparatively to literatures outside France, his basic substantiation does come, not surprisingly, from French literature and the French cultural complex. In some ways this produces a special case; in particular, his argument throughout the book that the "literary milieu" from which literary writers derive and the similar milieu from which audiences derive produces a closed "cultural circuit" is less applicable to the English situation, where literary change has borne considerable relation to expanding audiences. Our introduction therefore goes on to introduce further comparative material, to suggest how procedures of this kind would apply to English literature. We therefore retain his three main categories—of Production, Distribution and Consumption in literature—and offer some brief indications of what the analogous materials for England are, together with some suggestions for further lines of enquiry.[4]

II

Production

Literary production, says M. Escarpit, is the "manifestation of a community of writers" which has changed demographically, has undergone persistent repatterning, and has involved considerable change in the character of literature from generation to generation. M. Escarpit is concerned, in short, with the ecology of writers; and he takes up a stress on the 'literary generation' which has been a distinctive feature of French literary scholarship but which has earned little attention in England. The idea of 'generation' has perhaps three main uses in the study of literature; it helps to explain to us the way in which literature is the product not only of individuals but of literary groupings which have some community of attitude, value and perception, and which acquire the character of specialized segments of society that carry the weight of the literary function; it helps to explain the remarkable and difficult phenomenon of æsthetic change, those grand stylistic evolutions through which literature goes from time to time and by which an apparently living and vigorous body of writing produced in a society gives way to a writing created on totally different premises; and it helps, finally, to explain the odd fact that literature goes through periods of remarkable efflorescence and energy followed by periods of relative decline. In so brief an introduction to a new field, M. Escarpit cannot give much attention to the fact that these things can happen as a result of larger changes in consciousness and sensibility, thought and values, in the society at large; nor does he tackle the question of the relation between the æsthetic evolution of literature—its character as a developing body of inheritances changing according to obligations felt to be internal to the nature of art—and its evolution as a result of changing social uses for literature and the shifting of social consciousness.[5] But he does stress the way in which groups or 'teams' emerge to dominate taste, and so the way in which stylistic change is in part a factor of distillation of prevailing cultural possibilities and also of the acceptance of groups of writers either by a large, or else a culturally influential, readership.[6] He then goes on to elucidate the notion of 'cultural takeover' by looking at two main kinds of structure within his literary groupings or teams: their structure according to geographical origin, and their structure according to social origin.

The geographical origins of writers are important because they involve dramatizations of the relationship between different parts of a nation; when, for instance, in post-Civil War America, writing ceased to be dominated by New England and large numbers of writers emerged from Middle Western origins, the whole weight of American literary culture changed. Escarpit points out some similar interesting oscillations in French literature; the proportion of Parisian-born to provincial French writers was high in the seventeenth century, low in the eighteenth, and balanced out in the nineteenth. In England it has often been noted that a large proportion of our writers come from provincial origins and gradually make their way towards the capital, so dramatizing in their writing a tension between two sources of value: local values deriving from the material amidst which they grew up, and more sophisticated values applied to such material (a classical instance would be George Eliot's *Middlemarch*). The urban-rural interaction has proved to be a great source of literary creativity. M. Escarpit does not go into the question of why capitals should be such a lure to writers, and he does not discuss the increasing 'urbanization' of writers and literary perspectives. Nor does he consider in detail the role of Paris as a 'culture capital' for writers from many countries other than France, nor the character of the particular communities —for instance, the bohemian community—that have made it such. But he does suggest that the distribution of writers in the society is an important field of study—and that one factor in stylistic change is the way in which literary values tend to get renewed by the emergence of writers from new sectors, geographical and social, in the community. More intensive studies have been done on some aspects of his undertaking; see, for instance, Cesar Grana's admirable analysis, *Bohemian versus Bourgeois*, of the way in which bohemia was to a considerable extent a development of an influx of younger sons of the middle-classes into Paris at a time when both patronage and the possibilities of access to other professions were drying up.[7] In England, it has been noted, stylistic change is often linked to the emergence of large numbers of writers from minority sources in the culture, in response to the possibility of finding new ways of exploring the writer's relationship with his audience. Thus Raymond Williams comments in *The Long Revolution* about the period 1870 to 1950:

> It has been widely noted that an unusual proportion of the important imaginative literature of these years was written by people outside the majority English pattern. This had been true to some extent of the Victorian novel, but in these later years the relative importance of writers from abroad or from minority groups, as well as of women, is marked. Hardy, James, Shaw, Synge, Yeats, Eliot, Conrad, Lawrence, O'Casey, Joyce, Thomas compose a short list of some significance, not in the fact that, with the exception of the Irish, any particular minority is noticeable, but that difficult questions are raised about the majority pattern, the normal English mode, which certainly seems, in this period, relatively uncreative.[8]

The presence of a significant number of writers from minority sources in English culture can indeed be demonstrated for the last two centuries from the following table, which is derived from an analysis at present being conducted by the authors of this introduction into the literary class in England, and which uses as the basis of its sample the writers listed by George Watson in his *Concise Cambridge Bibliography of English Literature* (London,

TABLE ONE
ENGLISH AUTHORS FROM MINORITY SOURCES

19th Century

	Total sample	Irish	Scots	Welsh	Huguenot	Jewish	Immigrant	Emigrant
Novelists	32	6	3	0	1	1	1	2
Poets	36	2	2	0	0	0	2	6
Dramatists	6	0	0	0	1	1	0	0
Scholarly writers	15	0	0	0	0	1	0	0
Essayists	0	0	0	0	0	0	0	0

20th Century

	Total sample	Irish	Scots	Welsh	Huguenot	Jewish	Immigrant	Emigrant
Novelists	35	3	1	0	0	0	6	8
Poets	23	2	1	1	0	0	2	1
Dramatists	5	4	0	0	0	0	0	0
Scholarly writers	8	0	0	0	0	0	1	0
Essayists	7	2	0	0	0	0	1	1

revised ed., 1965. The minorities here are not of course provincial but derive from outside England as such; the category 'emigrant' refers to writers, whether English by origin or not, who at some point expatriated themselves, while the 'immigrant' category includes expatriates *to* England.

But while he suggests the presence of minority sources in the community of literary writers, M. Escarpit also emphasizes the degree to which, both in English and in French writing, there emerges in the nineteenth century a 'literary milieu'—a group somewhere near the centre of the social scale who tend to be the main representatives of literary activity as writers and as readers, and who increasingly tend therefore to 'appropriate' the activity of serious literature in the society. Again, the survey-in-progress by the present authors throws some light on the way this particular sector in society has developed as a literary class. In the following two tables, the selected, 'literary' writers of the *Concise Cambridge Bibliography* are examined over the last four centuries in the light of father's occupation and the author's education:

TABLE TWO

SOCIAL CLASS OF ENGLISH AUTHORS ASSESSED BY FATHER'S OCCUPATION

	17th and 18th cents.	19th cent.	20th cent
Aristocracy, upper middle class	28	16	14
Professional, merchant and business classes	33	62	35
Lower middle class (shopkeepers, clerks, schoolmasters, artisans)	26	15	9
Working class (small farmers, labourers)	8	9	3
Undetermined	3	2	—
TOTAL	98	104	61

TABLE THREE

SOCIAL CLASS OF ENGLISH AUTHORS ASSESSED BY EDUCATION

Private tutor	10	8	6
Public school (as terminal educ.)	7	9	5
University	91	53	(+P.S.)53*
			(+G.S.)14
Grammar school (as terminal educ.)	9	12	5
Dissenting academy	4	—	—
Little education	7	7	4
	128	89	87

* P.S.—Public School
G.S.—Grammar School

These figures are in fact consistent with those in two other surveys. Raymond Williams took a sample of about 350 writers born between 1470 and 1920 for a general social history of the English author; Richard Altick, challenging his methods, studied 1,100 writers between 1800 and 1935.[9] Both surveys, though with different weight and with a different notion of what constitutes 'literature', reinforce our own impression that the English writer through the nineteenth century and up to about 1945 was likely to be middle-class in origin, and probably from a professional family; that he was likely to have gone to a public school or a university and might very well have entered a professional occupation himself. Our own survey also suggests that the social and educational range of serious writers has actually tended to *narrow* until lately: this doubtless reflects the fact that the cultural resources, the motivation and the financial support for serious literature were becoming socially limited over a period when the amount of writing being produced was growing vastly. In short, while we may think of literature as being 'appropriated' by a small class, we can also think of it as being *sustained* in a difficult context by that class. The fact that, as we have seen, a number of writers tend to come from the ranks of the socially mobile, or slightly displaced, is not actually completely inconsistent with this. Writers often appear to be those slightly displaced *within* their class; indeed it is often their struggle to adapt to, or resist dominant values, that produces the matter, as well as probably the *fact*, of their literary endeavour.

Escarpit then turns briefly to the question of literary financing, and distinguishes two types: internal financing (royalties or sales of copyright) and external financing (patronage, private income, or other forms of self-financing such as double occupation). In England the records are fairly clear, and the facts can be found in studies like Edwin M. Miller, *The Professional Writer in Elizabethan England* (Cambridge, Mass., 1959), A. S. Collins, *Authorship in the Days of Johnson* (London, 1927) and *The Profession of Letters: 1780–1832* (London, 1928), and J. W. Saunders, *The Profession of English Letters* (London, 1964). In addition two valuable surveys, commissioned by the Society of Authors and written by Richard Findlater—*What Are Writers Worth? A Survey of Authorship* (London, 1963) and *The Book Writers: Who Are They?* (London, 1966)—bring the picture up to date. From this material two things are clear. First, the literary profession in England has always been characteristically oversubscribed, producing a long-term literary proletariat. The characteristic situation of post-patronage literature had been one of precarious livelihood. With the expansion of the book, the newspaper, and then of radio, film and television, the demand for writing has increased steadily over time; but it has normally been filled by aspirants well in excess of need. The literary profession has always been a trade as well as a profession; it does not select its entrants; and the basic—as opposed to the high— skills of writing, which are literacy and a certain tenacity, are not rare. Second, what is normally financed by the 'internal' system is not so much literature as writing generally. M. Escarpit emphasizes the importance of the notion of the writer's copyright possession of his work, a notion which makes it a saleable commodity. In England, this was defined by the Act for the Encouragement of Learning of 1709 and refined through subsequent legislation right through to the International Copyright Agreements of the later nineteenth century. Once established, it enabled writers to sell their copyrights, either on an outright or an edition basis, or through some form of subscription scheme. (So Gay earned £1,000 for his *Poems*, and Scott £4,200 for the *Lord of the Isles*, by selling their copyright; Matthew Prior earned £4,400 for his *Poems* and Pope some £5,000 for his *Iliad* by subscription sales.) By the end of the nineteenth century, with the emergence of literary agents and the Society of Authors, the uncertain situation of authorial financing was effectively stabilized in England on an advance-and-royalty pattern. Now under all such schemes large profits are potentially possible, especially with the growth of subsidiary rights from magazine publication, paperback publication, sale of foreign rights, film and television adaptation; and a small number of writers have been earning increasing profits. But the system simply gives financial advantage to the author who sells most copies, and the development of the public taste has been such that this rarely (at least in their lifetime) goes to writers who produce serious literary work. Some of the resulting difficulties have played an important part in English writing, and today in a period of inflation and a period of reduction of new literary titles among publishers they have become particularly noticeable. With the large expansion of the reading public at the end of the last century, the idea of the market produced increasing revulsion among writers of serious intent (see, for instance, George Gissing's *New Grub Street*), and the very definition of serious literature came to be, in effect, that work too arcane and difficult to satisfy the general reader: hence avant-gardism. As public taste has widened and high-cultural confidence has declined among writers and their primary audience, this sharp highbrow-lowbrow or élite-vulgar stratification has weakened. The fact remains that the market has rarely financed, especially in his early career, the serious writer; and forms of self- or other patronage have been necessary. Thus though the disappearance of patronage in the eighteenth century freed the writer from many obligations and allowed him greater freedom of appeal to an anonymous community of audiences, it did not produce a situation in which all serious literature could be financed directly from the market. Though a good many writers, including *some* who have produced serious literature (Scott, Tennyson and Bernard Shaw, for example), made large sums from the sale of their work, most literary careers not based on private income have been precarious. High rewards have normally depended, as Arnold Bennett admitted, on "strong mercantile interests", and the claims of trade have constantly competed in the mind of the English writer with the claims of 'literature'. Now, with the need for larger print-runs, the new literary book is becoming a shrinking item in the total book-market; with circulation of books held artificially low because of multiple borrowing from the excellent public library provision in Britain, the financing of authors has become a severe problem. Hence the appeals for supplementary financing of authors by Arts Council bursaries and for Public Lending Right. But the problem is even greater than this, because the main sale of much new literature is to libraries, and the total purchase of libraries is hardly sufficient to provide a large enough print-run for a new novel or book of poems. In this way, the 'literary' part of the market seems actually to be a declining part, in a period of commercial rationalization, concentration and rising costs.

Distribution

M. Escarpit's account of the emergence of the publisher as the main instrument of distribution, the obstetrician who selects, edits and transmits, is of sufficient general application to require very little modification. To his account might be added the all-important fact for the character of publishing and the book-trade in England, that the dominance of the English linguistic block to which he refers has meant that Britain has the benefit of a vastly greater number of titles and volume-sales than France. Where France publishes some 10–12,000 titles a year, Britain publishes now some 30,000 titles a year (as compared with 2,600 in 1850)—or something like 300 million actual copies, of which about half are exported. This gives Britain a large and expansive publishing industry, but one which, in order to cope with its export production, has had to reshape itself radically. Where, at the beginning of the century, there were a large number of small publishing houses with their distinctive 'collections' of authors of which M. Escarpit speaks, today the number of distinct firms have diminished as a result of mergers and takeovers, leaving large combines in control. Publishing is no longer the personal activity of educated gentlemen; it is a large-scale commercial operation which contributes greatly to the balance of payments. A large part of its activity is geared toward educational, scientific and technical publishing, and the book has increasingly become one of the media rather than a distinctively literary object. As a result of this process, the sense of personal community in the circuit composed of author, publisher and reader has considerably diminished.[10] From the author's point of view, both publisher and reader have become more remote. This sense of distance is increased by the fact that the bookshop is a declining outlet for the book; today, only a third of the books sold in England are sold in bookshops. Another third is bought by libraries and the remaining third by educational institutions. This suggests the growth of a large number of specialist audiences, using books mainly for purposes of information or educational advancement. In short, what Mr. Escarpit calls the 'cultured circuit' less and less dominates in the book-market. At the same time, the process of wider circulation which M. Escarpit refers to as 'blockade-running' (i.e. books reaching beyond the literary milieu formed by the circle of writers, publishers, reviewers and bookshops) has vastly extended. Since M. Escarpit wrote, we have seen the full spread of the 'paperback revolution', important not so much for the paperback format itself, but for the species of distribution used. From the penetration of the cheap book into newsagents and the setting up of station bookstalls in the nineteenth century to the presence of paperbacks in laundrettes and garages today, this process of distributive expansion has gone on in Britain. As the number of titles has increased (between 1960 and 1968 the number of titles increased sixfold to well over 30,000) the saturation of the market hopefully mentioned by M. Escarpit has more or less come about. So far, however, it is not clear (despite the claim made to this effect by Raymond Williams in *The Long Revolution*) that we now have a majority book-buying public; a survey by the Opinion Research Centre in 1967 suggested that only 25 per cent of the population bought paperbacks but that these bought them fairly regularly. Perhaps the most important effect of the situation is that the book has today lost its scarcity value. It is now a highly available (and in many respects a highly ephemeral) object. Nor, today, is the publisher exactly the administrator of scarcity by the selection of titles, as M. Escarpit suggests. And, even to the extent that he is, his role has been challenged by the ease of copying systems like duplication and xerox—which in the United States for example have totally transformed the situation in the world of small magazines, enabling writers to 'publish' whatever they like with ease and circulate their work freely though with little commercial profit. Today the problem for the literary book is to make its presence felt in the seamless web of communication.

Consumption

M. Escarpit's most challenging and interesting assumption in this section is the notion that the writer characteristically writes for a closed and selected world or else reaches out towards postulated foreign or future publics. This is a substantial insight and one essential to an effective sociology of literature. This leads him to the notion of creative treason as the clue to a book's continuing popularity; a book that appeals to posterity is a book that is capable of being revealed, sculptured and defaced by various use from various publics. It is with this conception that M. Escarpit is able to close off his circuit; the public makes the book makes the author, as well as vice versa.

What, then, distinguishes the literary work, as opposed to any other written document, is its non-functional nature. But that very situation tends to stratify audiences; the cultured audience (though it is different for every book) has a certain demographic unity, and the work of art touches on its special community assumptions. The group imposes a language, ideas, literary genres and forms upon the writer; style is not only the man but also the society. It is the groups who do not do this who lie outside the cultured circuit: who overhear literature rather than participate in it. M. Escarpit's argument is both extended and qualified by recent work that has been done in semiology, and especially that of Roland Barthes (see his *Writing Degree Zero* (London, 1967)), which argues that in fact the modern writers' languages have been pluralized by the presence of plural audiences with plural languages— producing, in effect, the æsthetic self-speculation of modernism. As a result of this sort of emphasis, some interesting work has developed lately in the discussion of 'registers' in literature. 'Register' refers to situational uses of language and the ways in which these are conventionalized; fiction, particularly, tends within the single work to use various registers taken from other forms of writing.[11] The fact that literary language and literary structure is a species of social perception is thus more complex than M. Escarpit makes it. In addition there are tactical problems about distinguishing between the 'unsigned' or public and the 'signed' or private features of literary works.

Nonetheless M. Escarpit is illuminating in his way of seeing that the act of publishing puts, in a post facto way, some of these aspects of literature to the test. The public cannot directly inter-

vene in what is already written; but they can intervene indirectly,
not only by reading (or not reading) a particular book, but also by
imposing myths upon it in order both to betray and to understand
it. The reader socializes the work; and since he uses reading in
many different ways he may socialize different books very dif-
ferently. In stressing this, M. Escarpit encourages us to move
beyond the normal content analysis approach to the study of
literature or works in the media. Most of this work has tended to
assume a consonance between the values of the author and those
of the reader or viewer; it therefore inevitably functions best with
forms of mass-expression like best-sellers or comic strips, where
the popularity is proven and it is possible to make hypotheses
about the basis of the general appeal. M. Escarpit, in separating
the category of 'escape-literature' and 'escape-reading', probably
over-simplifies; but he is perfectly right to stress that where literature is concerned, a much more complex set of inter-relationships
is set up. Even serious reading can be a form of withdrawal as well
as of genuine intensification; and the role of connoisseur of literature can well be a social role—one which itself merits social analysis.
As he suggests, one of the most valid ways of examining literature
culturally or sociologically is by exploring the interactions between
the intentions of the writer and the intentions of the reader—considering the latter both as an individual affected by the characteristic modern limitations on his reading-time and his reading-purpose
and as part of an influential group. The fact that a large part of
the activity of literature now goes on as some aspect of education—
much of our contemporary reading, in an age of maximum economic use of persons, is done in the categorized reading period of the
'educational' stage of one's life; an enormous proportion of our
books find their way into one or another educational context—is a
highly significant indicator of the nature and status of 'literature'
today.

III

The particular value of *The Sociology of Literature* is, then,
that it is an intensive, suggestive and coherent study of a particular
complex of literary action in society. Our introduction is intended
to suggest the seminal nature of the analysis and the fact that,
within its highly economical and brief framework, it raises
numerous matters that might elicit further study. Though quite
heavily documented, it is more than a documentary account of the
existence of literature in society; indeed documentary accounts of
writing and the book-trade are not, in fact, new. The novelty of

M. Escarpit's book has lain in the fact that for the first time disparate data, accumulated by many literary scholars, has seemed capable of being drawn together into an overall scheme. To some extent the scheme, or model, is too tight and constricting, and is subject to criticism from the standpoint of both the sociologist and the literary critic. The sociologist, for instance, would doubtless like to see more room made in the discussion for consideration of broader social forces. (For example, over the last two centuries occupational groups of many kinds have sought increasing self-identification and protection; the professionalism of writers, on which M. Escarpit touches, is but one aspect of a broader professionalization. And not just in this way but in many others the writer is subject to large forces of social change, to alterations in his role and his function, which merit fuller analysis.) The literary critic, in turn, would want to see how such changes affected the nature of the literary text itself: to examine the changes in language, artistic structure, and style, often of an intensely complex kind, that occur in the evolution of art and can be assumed to have certain social causes. He would, also, probably, question the way in which the terminology of the market is made to dominate every literary transaction. Nonetheless the entire area of study has undoubtedly been significantly advanced by M. Escarpit's brief, invigorating and seminal book.

Malcolm Bradbury

1970   Bryan Wilson

NOTES

1 See, for instance, the work of Leo Lowenthal, in *Literature and the Image of Man* (Boston, Mass., 1957) and *Literature, Popular Culture, and Society* (Englewood Cliffs, N.J., 1961), and that of Philip Rieff, in *The Triumph of the Therapeutic* (New York and London, 1966), for fully developed sociological approaches to literary and cultural matters.

2 F. R. Leavis's comments on this subject occur in two essays, "Literature and Society" and "The Sociology of Literature", reprinted in *The Common Pursuit* (London, 1952).

3 Malcolm Bradbury, "Literature and Sociology", in *Essays and Studies 1970*, ed. A. R. Humphreys (London, 1970).

4 The following sections draw considerably on material developed at much greater length and with greater analytical detail in Malcolm Bradbury, *The Social Context of Modern English Literature* (Oxford, 1971). The reader who wishes to follow these matters further is referred particularly to the sections on "The Writer Today", "Communications" and "The Culture". We also draw on as-yet-unpublished material from a book in progress by the two present authors.

5 For this broader emphasis, see the book by Malcolm Bradbury cited above.

6 Along these lines, there are two extremely interesting analyses of the rise of a literary form in England seen in the light of the significant

audience: these are L. C. Knights, *Drama and Society in the Age of Jonson* (London, 1937), and Ian Watt, *The Rise of the Novel* (London, 1947).

7 Cesar Grana, *Bohemian Versus Bourgeois: French Society and the French Man of Letters in the Nineteenth Century* (New York and London, 1964). (The paperback edition is titled: *Modernity and Its Discontents*.)

8 Raymond Williams, *The Long Revolution* (London, 1961). Quotation from p. 265 of the Penguin paperback edition.

9 Raymond Williams, "The Social History of English Writers", Part 2, Chapter 5 of *The Long Revolution* (London, 1961); and Richard D. Altick, "The Sociology of Authorship: The Social Origins, Education and Occupations of 1,100 British Writers, 1800–1935", *The Bulletin of the New York Public Library*, LXVI, vi (June 1962), 389–404. Both are well worth consulting since they offer much more intensive analysis than does Escarpit of the meaning of the social backgrounds of writers. For a more general view, see J. W. Saunders, *The Profession of English Letters* (London, 1964).

10 A much fuller record of developments in British book-publishing in this century is to be found in R. J. L. Kingsford, *The Publishers Association: 1896–1946* (London, 1970). Other studies of the British book-trade of major importance are H. S. Bennett, *English Books and Readers* (London, 3 volumes, 1952–70), covering Caxton to 1640, and Richard D. Altick, *The English Common Reader: A Social History of the Mass Reading Public: 1800–1900* (Chicago and London, 1957). All these books are, of course, illuminating for the topic Escarpit moves to in his following section, on 'Consumption', as well.

11 An interesting discussion of this topic occurs in Jonathan Raban, *Techniques of Modern Fiction* (London, 1968), Chapter 12.

CONTENTS

PART FOUR

CONSUMPTION

Translator's Note

Readers have long been accustomed to a traditional approach to literature which seeks to interpret a literary work as an entity unrelated to both the writer's life and his environment. Even the literary purist, however, is aware of the social conditions surrounding the birth, distribution and consumption of any given work. Literary sociology attempts to discern and describe these conditions.

Sociology of literature is a proper name for the study of the origin, history and constitution of literary society, but it does not by any means circumscribe all the elements from which it draws. For literary sociology can explain literature only with the assistance of related disciplines such as economics, psychology, history and philosophy.

To categorize such a science is difficult. It belongs to the realm of comparative literature only if we use that term in its broadest sense, for it does not incorporate the study of influences, of translations or of the fortunes of traditional themes such as Hamlet or Faust. It does concern itself, however, with the lives of authors. How can we hope to understand fully Voltaire's works if we are ignorant of his knowledge of the English people, their customs and their language? Literary sociology is a science of its own, dealing with the effects of men on books and books on men.

Although a young science, literary sociology has already achieved a considerable following in France, where it has begun to flourish under the leadership of such men as Robert Escarpit. In the United States, however, there are few scholars who have undertaken studies along the lines described in *Sociology of Literature*; among them are Henri Peyre, René Wellek, Austin Warren, Richard Altick and the late David T. Pottinger. One hopes that a determined effort to unravel the social conditions inherent in any manifestation of literature will take place here as well. The field is wide open.

Professor Robert Escarpit, Chairman of the Department of Comparative Literature at Bordeaux, has long studied comparative literature and literary sociology. After World War

II, during which he served both in the army and the Resistance and was awarded the *Croix de guerre,* he received the Doctorat-ès-lettres in 1952. Since then he has published prolifically — from *L'Angleterre dans l'oeuvre de Madame de Staël* (1954), a critical work, to *Le Littératron* (1964), a novel. In that space of time, he has written six novels and seven critical works, and has contributed articles to the *Encyclopedia Britannica* on Madame de Staël and Benjamin Constant, and to the *Encyclopédie française* on English literature and the sociology of literature.

Professor Escarpit is known to millions of newspaper readers in France who have seen his daily article in *Le Monde.* Soon many of the more than 1800 articles he has contributed will be gathered and republished in book form.

At present, along with his other responsibilities, Professor Escarpit is the scientific director of the *International Dictionary of Literary Terms* and director of the *Centre de Sociology des faits littéraires* in Bordeaux, where he continues research into the new-born sociology of literature.

Sociology of Literature was published in France in 1958. It is now in its second edition there and has been translated into German, Japanese, Spanish and Burmese, while excerpts have appeared in Slavic languages.

The sociological study of literature has led to a new vocabulary, often technical in nature, for which we have only approximate equivalents in English. Elusive words and ideas which may seem vague at first will become clearer as one reads the text. Some of these are *fait littéraire, public-milieu, public-interlocuteur, circuit lettré, circuit populaire* and *aptitude à la gratuité.*

The translation into English of this work was begun in 1962 and owes its completion to the good will, patience, efforts and intelligence of many people, among them Professor Escarpit, who answered countless questions in interviews and by mail, and the editors of the *Lake Erie College Studies,* Professors William Peterson, Marjorie Johnson and Robert Nugent. I also wish to express my gratitude to Richard Morton of McMaster University and to my wife, Janine Pick, who proofread this work and supplied encouragement throughout.

1965   E.P.

Sociology
of
Literature

PART ONE

Principles and Methods

CHAPTER I

Why a Sociology of Literature?

Literature and Society

E ACH AND EVERY literary fact presupposes a writer, a book and a reader; or, in general terms, an author, a product and a public. By way of an extremely complex transmitting mechanism, a circuit of interrelationships is constituted. It combines art, technology and business, uniting well-defined individuals in a more or less anonymous though limited community.

The presence of artists poses psychological, moral and philosophic problems at all points of the circuit; their work raises esthetic, stylistic, linguistic and technical problems. Finally, the existence of a public implies historical, political, social and even economic problems. In other words, there are at least a thousand and one ways of exploring any literary fact.

It is difficult to study the threefold relationship of literature to individuals, to abstract forms and to diverse situations. It is not easy to picture tri-dimensional phenomena, especially when asked to write their history. For centuries, literary history has held— and still holds fast— to the study only of particular writers and their works, to a biographical and textual commentary. It has considered the aggregate context as a sort of decoration best left to the inquisitive mind of the political historian.

The absence of a real sociological perspective is evident in even the best traditional textbooks of literary history. Writers/are sometimes conscious of a social dimension which they try to represent, but, lacking a rigorous method adapted to that end, they often remain immured in the classical framework of the man and his work. On such a two-dimensional screen the perspectives of history are obscured. Literary facts undergo distortions comparable to those of a world map which has no relief; as a map drawn by a schoolboy falsely shows an enormous Alaska overshadowing a tiny Mexico, so do twelve or fifteen years of Versailles in the seventeenth century overshadow sixty years of French literary life.

Those difficulties will never be completely eliminated. Even were a perfect delineation possible, it is essential that explorers of literature, whether biographers or commentators, historians or critics, attain a complete and undistorted view of all literary facts. If we wish to understand writers in our time, we cannot forget that writing is a profession— or at least a lucrative activity— practiced within the framework of economic systems which exert undeniable influences on creativity. We cannot forget, if we wish to understand literature, that a book is a manufactured product, commercially distributed and thus subject to the laws of supply and demand. We must see that literature is, among other things, incontestably, the production segment of the book industry, as reading is its consumption segment.

An Historical Account

Our notion of literature is recent and dates from the last years of the eighteenth century. Originally, we did not *make* literature; we *had* it. It was the distinguishing sign of well-educated people: for this notion we have substituted that of "general culture." For a contemporary of Voltaire, however, the world of "literature" opposed the world of the "public," or the people. This situation implies a cultural aristocracy and as a result, the problem of social relations between literature and society could scarcely emerge into consciousness.

An evolution began in the sixteenth century which picked up momentum in the eighteenth. On the one hand, knowledge became specialized; scientific and technical works tended to be progressively shut off from real literature, while the scope of literature diminished and tended to be restricted to that of a pastime. Doomed to this unwarranted position, literature tried to establish new organic relationships between itself and the community. What one may call "engaged" literature is the last of these attempts.

On the other hand, the same technical and cultural progress which accentuated the gratuitousness of literature enlarged the need for literature and increased the efficiency of communication between the consuming public and the book industry. With the invention of the printing press, the development of the book trade, the decline of illiteracy and, later, with the advent of audio-visual techniques, what used to be the privileged characteristics of an upper class of well-educated people became the cultural occupation of a relatively unrestricted middle-class élite. Then, in recent times, these became the way to improve the masses intellectually.

Both specialization and this wider distribution reached their critical points in the early eighteen hundreds. At that time, literature began to appreciate its social dimension. *De la littérature considérée dans ses rapports avec les institutions sociales*, by Madame de Staël, published in 1800, is doubtless the first attempt in France to join literature and society in a systematic study.

Madame de Staël defines her intentions in her prefatory discourse:

> I have undertaken the examination of what are the influences of religion, morals and laws on our literature, and of what is the influence of literature on religion, morals and laws.[1]

This undertaking extends to literature Montesquieu's treatment of the history of law: Madame de Staël, one of his intellectual disciples, wrote a *Spirit of Literature*. At a time when the words "modern" and "national" took on new meaning in the critics' vocabulary, an explanation of the diversity of literature in time and space by the variations and peculiar traits of human societies became inevitable.

The *Zeitgeist*, the spirit of an era, and the *Volksgeist*, the national spirit, were the two fundamental notions which appeared and took shape in Madame de Staël's circle of German friends. They are found again in the doctrine of Taine, divided according to the ternary formula of *race*, *milieu* and *moment*. The convergence of these three factors determines the literary phenomenon.

Taine lacked a clear idea of "human science." Half a century after him, Georges Lanson criticized this deficiency: "The analysis of poetic genius has nothing in common with the analysis of sugar but the name."[2] Taine's outline of *race*, *milieu*, and *moment* is too unpolished to embrace all the aspects of an infinitely complex reality. Above all, his methods are not adapted to the specificity of the literary fact: beyond some brutally transposed procedures from nature and science, he has access only to traditional methods of history and literary criticism (biographical analysis and textual commentary) with which to approach the material he is studying.

Yet the essence of Taine's doctrine survives. After Taine, neither historians nor critics could allow themselves — although they did sometimes— to ignore the fact that external

---

1. *De la littérature,* "Discours préliminaire," Paragraph 1.
2. "Méthodes de l'histoire littéraire," *Etudes Françaises,* Premier Cahier (January 1925), p. 23.

circumstances, notably social ones, have a bearing on literary activities.

Economics being a human science, more efficacy could have been expected from Marxism than from Taine's doctrine. The first Marxist theories, however, showed themselves to be extremely discreet on literary questions. The volume *Sur la littérature et sur l'art*, in which the writings of Marx and Engels appear jointly, is rather disappointing. It is only with Plekhanov, in the beginning of this century, that a real Marxist theory of literature is constructed, and it, of course, was sociological in nature. But later, anxiety for political efficiency led Soviet literary critics (and with them, Communist critics) to put less accent on literature than on social observation gleaned from literary works.

Vladimir Zhdanov defined his attitude in 1956:

Literature must be considered in its inseparable relation to social life, the background of those historical and social factors which influence the writer: this has always been the governing principle behind Soviet literary research. It is founded on the Marxist-Leninist method of perception and analysis of reality, and it excludes the subjective and arbitrary point of view which considers each book as an independent and isolated entity. Literature is a social phenomenon, the perception of reality through creative imagery.[3]

The methodological consequence of this attitude is obvious:

The principle of the historical method which is at the base of Soviet literary research has as its primary criterion for all works of art the degree of fidelity with which it represents reality in all its complexity.[4]

While the literary sociology applied by the Hungarian Georges Lucas and his disciple, the Frenchman Lucien Goldmann, also bears the Marxist stamp, it is perhaps less rigorous but more conscious of specifically esthetic problems.

The principal opposition to the Soviet sociological method was "formalism." The powerful formalist school, officially condemned in the nineteen-thirties, sought to apply a

---

3. "Some Recent Soviet Studies in Literature," *Soviet Literature*, No. 8 (Moscow, 1956), p. 141
4. *Ibid.*

science of esthetics to the forms and procedures of literary art.[5] In fact, it was only one aspect of a vast movement which had its origins in Germany and in which were combined the influences of Wilhelm Dilthey's neo-Hegelian philosophy, of philological criticism, and of *Gestalt* psychology. Throughout the world this *Literaturwissenschaft* or science of literature has been, from the nineteenth century up to our own time, one of the most serious obstacles to the appearance of a real sociology of literature.

The science of sociology, however, through Comte, Spencer, Le Play, Durkheim and others progressed towards complete autonomy. It bypassed literature, that complex domain of extremely uncertain data and definitions, for literature had been protected by an attitude of deference.

Sociological tendencies were expressed throughout the last half-century in the form of great, governing ideas, rather than in the form of one coherent method. They have sometimes joined with formalistic tendencies: L. L. Schüking and the sociology of taste, R. Wellek and the study of language as a social element in literature.[6] Comparative literature, the last-born of the literary sciences, has undoubtedly initiated the greatest number of interesting ideas.

The study of the huge theme of a collective consciousness, to which Paul Hazard devoted part of his work,[7] leads to that "history of ideas" which Lovejoy has made his specialty and which is now indispensable to a full understanding of literature. Jean-Marie Carré has oriented his pupils towards the problem of "mirages," a problem raised by the distorted view which one national group obtains of another through the influence of writers.[8]

Among governing ideas, one of the most fecund was certainly that of "generations." This idea was expressed in 1920 by François Mentré in his work, *Les générations sociales*. But the merit of being the first to elaborate this idea belongs to

5. Let us note, however, that between 1927 and 1930 there existed a "formalistic" sociology of literature. See Gleb Struve, *Histoire de la littérature soviétique* (Paris, 1946), pp. 226-229.

6. L. L. Schüking, *Die Soziologie der literarischen Geschmäcksbildung* (Leipzig, 1931). René Wellek and Austin Warren, *Theory of Literature* (New York, 1949).

7. *La crise de la conscience européenne* (Paris, 1935).

8. *Les écrivains français et le mirage allemand* (Paris, 1947).

Albert Thibaudet, whose revolutionary work, *Histoire de la littérature française de 1789 à nos jours*, appeared in 1937. It was the fundamental work by Henri Peyre, *Les générations littéraires*, published in 1948, which really demonstrated the sociological significance of "this problem of collective inspiration which is that of literary generations."[9] To these names one might add that of Guy Michaud; in his *Introduction à une science de la littérature*, which appeared in Istanbul in 1950, he was the first to launch explicitly— among a hundred other ideas— the idea of a literary sociology as we understand the term today.

Up to recent times, however, the absence of documentation made the *in vivo* study of sociological phenomena in literature practically impossible. How could one pretend to interpret the past when incapable of checking facts in the present? Fortunately, this situation has rapidly been improved in the ten years which followed the Second World War.

One must first mention the decisive role played by UNESCO: systematic censuses taken by its various divisions permitted the acquisition of previously inaccessible information about collective aspects of literature. In 1956, R. E. Barker's report, *Books For All*, although too fragmentary and conjectural in documentation, was nevertheless useful as a basis for work to come.

The book industry also timidly investigated standardization and market studies. I must regretfully say that the superstition of a "sixth sense" and, more particularly, commercial caution make France one of the most backward countries in accumulating information. The only official documentation on the book trade in France, excellent but desperately thin, is the *Monographie de l'édition* by Pierre Monnet, published in 1956 by the Cercle de la Librairie.[10] In 1960, The National Union of Publishers asked the Institute of Economic and Social Research to investigate reading and book practices in France. The very important results of this investigation have not been published commercially.[11] German publishers and bookstores regularly publish precise and

---

9. Henri Peyre, *Les générations littéraires* (Paris, 1948). It was Henri Peyre who, in 1950, urged me to undertake research in the sociology of literature.

10. First edition (1956), Second edition (1959), Third edition (1963).

11. See the bibliography at the end of this chapter.

abundant documentation under the title *Buch und Buchhandel in Zahlen*. In England, uncontested capital of the "capitalist" edition, partial studies are already numerous. This situation also prevails in new countries which are trying to make up their cultural lag (and are succeeding in their efforts) with the help of an intelligently planned book trade policy.

Thus we come to what in our time and the future will undoubtedly be the most efficient apparatus for research in literary sociology: namely, the necessity for planning in the book trade industry.

Towards a Book Industry Policy

What used to be the quest for individual wisdom, an attempt at self-knowledge, is now the search for aggregate wisdom. In literature, our societies seem, as a rule, to lack self-knowledge. The advancement of the masses, foretold over a century ago and now an inexorable reality in the last generation, has scarcely led to a rethinking of the material characteristics of political communities. Cultural traits have been neglected to a larger extent. Even though we talk a great deal about it, the notion of mass culture remains marked by a paternalistic and missionary zeal which masks its real lack of force. Thus a community of one million men has at its disposal a literary culture meant for a community of thousands.

So it is not surprising that this situation has troubled organizations interested in social welfare. In January of 1957, the magazine *Informations Sociales*, the organ of the "Union Nationale des caisses d'allocations familiales," devoted a special issue to a vast poll on "literature and the mass audience." The poll had the merit of bringing into the forefront almost all the problems of literary sociology, and its publication may be considered as a decisive step towards regulated research.[12]

An article by Gilbert Mury, "Is a Sociology of the Book Trade Possible?" is notable in that it justifies literary so-

---

12. The poll was based on a series of observations of unequal value. At the request of René Mongé, editor-in-chief of the magazine and initiator of the poll, I coordinated the results and commented on them.

7

ciology through the example of religious sociology. Deference to human values retarded the appearance of literary sociology and directly opposed religious sociology. But the same need to act, to elaborate a coherent design, which has always permitted believers to conquer their scruples, must conquer the reticence of literary purists.

Not so long ago, all objective research on faith and religious practices was considered by excellent minds as an attack against mysticism. Today the Catholic episcopate is beginning such investigations in order to adapt itself to the reality of its pastoral movement . . . . It is certain that, from writers to book dealers, all men connected with the book trade would gain from the results of systematic studies of the public and, consequently, they would better envision new ways of reaching them.[13]

Gilbert Mury reminds us that salesmen have their place in the Temple of the Muses: having economic aspects which religion wishes to ignore, literature must be all the more open to sociological considerations. To see clearly is not simply a necessary action, it is also good business. But we need not necessarily limit ourselves to commercial considerations. Diderot writes in his "Lettre sur le commerce de la librairie:"

A blunder which is always committed by those whose lives are governed by general maxims is the application of the manufacture of material to the publishing industry.

The sociology of literature must respect the specific nature of the literary fact. The tradesman may use literary sociology to his advantage, but it may also aid the reader by assisting traditional literary science, whether historical or critical, in the tasks which belong to it. These preoccupations remain indirectly those of literary sociology, but its role is only to express them at the social level.

Such a program demands vast research which surpasses the capacity of individuals or even of isolated groups. In the first edition of this book, published in 1958, I was able to present only a few results of a miniscule part of the stated

---

13. *Informations sociales* (January 1947), p. 64. Gilbert Mury, a professor of philosophy, is presently engaged in research on literary sociology dealing mainly with the behavior of the public.

problems. But that edition permitted me to enter into contact with researchers who shared my interest in the same problems and even to awaken enough curiosity to begin new research. Several publications have devoted space to this rereach;[14] various conferences have shown that specialists of criticism or literary history are adopting the sociological perspective more and more willingly.

There is now in Bordeaux a Center of Sociological Literary Facts and another is being created in Brussels. With the help of Penguin Books an institute of a similar nature has been founded in Birmingham. Encouraging response has been received from America, Germany, Italy, Japan, Africa and the socialist countries. An authentic sociology of literature is being born.

---

14. *Tendances*, No. 1 (1959). *Chronique sociale de France*, No. 1 (1959). *Esprit*, No. 4 (1960), etc.

Bibliography

Altick, R. D., *The English Common Reader*, Chicago, 1956.

Angoulvent, P., *L'Edition française au pied du mur*, Paris, 1960.

Dumazedier, J. and Hassenforder, J., *Eléments pour une sociologie comparée de la production, de la diffusion et de l'utilisation du livre*, Bibliographie de la France, Paris, 1963.

Escarpit, R., "Les Méthodes de la sociologie littéraire," *Actes du 11e Congrès de l'Association internationale de Littérature Comparée*, Chapel Hill, North Carolina, 1958.

————, "La sociologie de la littérature," Encyclopédie française, Vol. XVII, 1963.

————, " 'Creative Treason' as a Key to Literature," *Yearbook of Comparative and General Literature*, #10, 1961.

Lough, J., *English Theatre Audiences in the 17th and 18th Centuries*, London, 1957.

Lukacs, G., *Literatur-Soziologie*, Neuwied, 1961.

Monnet, P., *Monographie de l'Edition*, Paris, 1956.

Pichois, C., "Vers une sociologie historique des faits littéraires," *Revue d'Histoire littéraire de la France*, 1961, #1.

Pottinger, D. T., *The French Book Trade in the Ancient Regime*, Harvard, 1958.

Schücking, L.L., *Die Soziologie der literarischen Geschmäcksbildung*, Leipzig, 1931.

Wellek, R., and Warren, A., *Theory of Literature*, New York, 1949.

"Littérature et grand public," *Informations sociales*, 1957, #1.
"Etudes sur la lecture et le livre en France," *Syndicat national des Editeurs*, Paris, 1960.

CHAPTER II

How is the Literary Fact Approached?

The Book, Reading and Literature

WE ARE MADE aware of the literary fact, principally, in three ways: by the book, by reading and by literature. In current usage we often employ one of these words when we mean another. However, these three notions are only partially similar, and the limits of each are not precise.

To define a book is a difficult undertaking. The only nearly complete definition to this day is so vague that it is not usable: "Bulk of a certain substance and dimension, sometimes folded or wound, on which are conveyed representative signs of certain intellectual data."[1] Littré hesitates between a material definition, "the union of several printed pages or manuscript pages," and a half-intellectual one, "work of the mind, either in prose or in verse, large enough to make at least a volume." The definition of the word *volume*, "a bound or sewn book," is of no assistance at all.

Actually, no universal definition of a book exists. Each country, each government, has its own definition. In France, the Minister of Commerce has one for customs and another for the treasury. UNESCO proposed a universal, statistical definition which would distinguish a book from a periodical. A book is a "non-periodical publication containing at least forty-nine pages." But Lebanon and South Africa demand fifty, Denmark sixty, Hungary sixty-four, Ireland, Italy and Monaco require one hundred! At the other end of the scale, Belgium is happy with forty, Czechoslovakia with thirty-two, Iceland with seventeen. As for India, the slightest brochure is considered a book! The United Kingdom's definition is a

---

1. This definition by Paul Otlet is quoted by Eric de Grolier in his *Histoire du livre*, *"Que sais-je?"* No. 620.

financial one: a book is any publication the price of which is at least sixpence.[2]

The fault of all of these definitions resides in their outlook; they consider the book to be a material object, not a means of cultural exchange. Many of them would include a railroad timetable, but would exclude certain scholastic editions of plays by Racine and Molière. And if some of these definitions take into account the contents of a book, it is curious that none considers its use. But a book is a "thing to read" and reading itself defines it.

Copied, printed or photographed, a book has as its goal the *multiplication* of words as well as their preservation. A book for one person would have no meaning. Thus it seems that the number of its readers should be included in any definition of a book. Statistically, however, only the title of a book is counted as a unit, not copies or editions of the work. No reference to the number of copies printed is made in official surveys.

Statistics published in different countries must thus be observed with extreme circumspection. Take, for example, some statistics for 1961. It appears that the "giants of production," those countries having published more than 10,000 titles, are six in number: the U.S.S.R. (73,999), the United Kingdom (24,893), Japan (24,223), West Germany (21,877), the United States (18,060), and France (12,705). This list is ridiculous. The margin by which the U.S.S.R. leads should be cut in half, as only 43,822 of its titles can properly be considered as books. The remainder are distributed free. Japan, with only 12,293 original publications, should be placed after Germany, which has 17,090. Finally, Italy, which defines a book too rigorously (at least 100 pages), should be advanced at least to the level of France, and perhaps slightly higher.[3]

If we take into account imports (translated works) and repeated listings (multiple translations, as in the U.S.S.R.), statistics by titles can indicate more or less the wealth and variety of the intellectual life of a country. They allow us

---

2. According to R. E. Barker, *Books For All*, p. 17.
3. *Ibid.* We should mention that the number given for the United States includes books put on sale commercially and does not include government publications distributed by the Administration. In the land of paperwork, these represent a considerable volume.

to estimate very roughly the amount and output of its writers, but cannot give us any idea of the importance of reading in its social life.

To analyze the phenomenon of reading, it is necessary to calculate not only the size of editions but also the size of impressions. These latter figures are generally known; the others are often obtained with more difficulty.

One may, however, acquire some idea of what is happening by examining the amount of paper consumed in each country. A new classification of countries according to that data, taking into account not only the per capita consumption of newspapers but also of paper consumed for writing and printing, would be of value. This would enable us to find that our six leaders are still frontrunners, but now the Netherlands, Switzerland, Belgium and the Scandinavian countries would join them. Great Britain and the U.S.S.R. would definitely take first place.[4]

Comparison of the book industry with the newspaper trade is significant. In France in 1955, of 10.6 kilograms of paper for writing and printing consumed per capita, the book industry's consumption was roughly 1.4 kilograms. That year, the newspaper industry consumed 9.2 kilograms per capita. But the number of words in a printed newspaper is, given the same weight and taking typographical habits into account, larger by one half than that in books. So one can safely say that the amount of reading material at the French reader's disposal in newspapers is roughly ten times larger than that in books. This proportion is valid for most Western European countries, although in the United Kingdom it is twelve to thirteen times greater. But in the U.S.S.R., available newspaper reading is only four times larger than that in books, while in the United States, the proportion is two hundred to one. Even should one deduct the space absorbed by prolix publicity, he may assign an honorable rank to Americans as readers of magazines, but not of books.

All possible reading material can not be taken at face value. If we consider the quantity of paper indicated above —eliminating illiterates and children while taking into ac-

---

4. *L'information à travers le monde*, U.N.E.S.C.O. (Paris, 1951), and "Papier d'impression et papier d'écriture," *Cahiers du centre de documentation de l'UNESCO*. (March 1954), 11.

count that the same material may be used by three or four readers— we should have to admit that a Frenchman reads 40,000 words a day on the average (or one and a half times the number in a book such as this), and an Englishman reads three times more than a Frenchman!

One should also include unsold books and exports in these calculations. Both factors tend to reduce the importance of the book in reading. In fact, the periodicity of newspapers and their ephemeral character make it both possible and necessary to adapt the volume of the edition to its sale, in order to avoid financial loss. Yet, it is particularly books which are exported. For France, exports represent from twenty to twenty-five per cent of the total of the book industry sales, or six billion francs each year (in 1954). However, France imports about two and a half billion francs' worth of books each year. Thus, of the total national production, from twelve to fifteen per cent is not consumed in France.[5]

One can see that books represent only a small part of possible reading materials and that effective reading of books is even smaller. However, as soon as the notion of literature intervenes, books take on another significance.

One should understand that literature cannot be defined through any qualitative criterion. My criterion is what I will call the "search for gratuitousness." Any work which is not functional, but an end in itself, is literature. Each act of reading which is not a means to an end, one which satisfies a cultural, non-utilitarian need, is literature.

Today, most reading is functional, notably that of newspapers in which we seek mainly information or documentation. But neither can all books be classified as literature.

Literature is but one of ten large categories in the decimal classification invented eighty years ago by the American librarian, Melvil Dewey, and adopted by most countries in their libraries:

0. General
1. Philosophy
2. Religion
3. Social Sciences
4. Philology
5. Pure Sciences
6. Applied Sciences
7. Arts and Amusements
8. Literature
9. History and Geography

5. Taken from R. E. Barker and Pierre Monnet.

Unfortunately, these categories are not precise. France, in particular, does not use the fourth category (Philology) which it adds, under the name of Linguistics, to the eighth category (Literature). Evidently, the label "Literature" includes the most diverse and sometimes the least literary articles.

This inclusiveness is the reason that official statistics can give only vague and often erroneous indications. If one holds to the decimal classification by titles, literature represents from thirty to thirty-five per cent of the French book trade. With slight variations, this proportion is common in highly productive countries—slightly smaller in Germany, slightly larger in English-speaking countries. Greece, with eighty per cent, is exceptional and makes one think that the present criteria of classification used in that country might be revised. On the contrary, proportions under thirty per cent are numerous. They fall even below ten per cent in newly-independent countries which previously were colonies. In these countries technical necessities rank first and autochthonous groups of writers have not as yet been able to develop.

Periodical publications, in particular those printed weekly and monthly, contain a variable but often rather large proportion of non-functional reading of a literary nature, such as serialized novels, short stories and essays. A portion of this material is re-issued later in book form, but often the amount of periodic literature is extensive and sometimes equals that in books. Without considering digests, articles published by such magazines as the *Saturday Evening Post* satisfy the literary needs of millions in place of books.

We cannot rely on formal classifications or systematic materials to obtain a clear idea of the relation between literature and reading. It is rather the nature of the author-public exchange which may help us to say what literature is— and what it is not. A large number of writings are functional in intention but are generally used in a non-fictional and literary way. These occur in newspapers and periodicals as well as in books, often in reporting and in book reviews. But one can readily cite numerous technical, scientific or philosophic works whose intention is literary and which have been accepted as such by the public. To the extent that any reading allows one to escape himself or to dream, or, on the contrary, to meditate or to cultivate himself without any specific aim, it may be literature: G. K. Chesterton has even shown that there is a literary use for railroad time-tables.[6]

6. See *The Man Who Was Thursday*, Chapter 1.

Conversely, there are non-literary uses of literary works: the consumption of literary works is not identical with literary reading. A book may be bought with other intentions than drawing either esthetic pleasure or cultural benefits from it.

Thus, the attempt to comprehend the literary fact— whatever the means used— raises problems of individual and collective behavior. A rigid definition of literature presupposes a convergence of intentions between reader and author; a broader definition demands at least a compatibility of intentions. If we do not recognize these requisites, it will be impossible for us to understand reading as anything else but the mechanical consumption of certain printed matter; it will be equally impossible for us to perceive in books anything but one of the forms of that matter, and certainly not the most important one.

Methods of Approach

The most obvious way to understand both a collective and psychological phenomenon is to ask questions of a sufficient number of judiciously chosen persons. Dr. Kinsey employed this method in his polls when he attempted to define the sexual behavior of his fellow Americans. He most certainly would have encountered many more difficulties had he tried to define their cultural behavior through the same process. The likelihood of lucid and sincere answers is extremely reduced as soon as someone's reading habits are examined. While the confession of one's sexual peculiarities may flatter a latent exhibitionist, the avowal of literary or anti-literary tastes (whether too undiscriminating or too refined) which lower one's position in society can only be painful. Most people find great difficulty in confessing to themselves the nature of their taste.

The comparison of data obtained by direct and systematic observation of the cultural comportment of one person with data which he himself supplies, even in good faith, enables one to understand the extreme difficulty of using subjective information. He who cites Stendhal or Malraux as customary reading and who confides that he sometimes reads a detective novel or two to relax, will hardly admit that the time he devotes to detective novels is several times greater than the time he gives his "bedside" books. If he mentions newspapers, he will forget the few minutes he spends looking at the comic strips which, accumulated, represent an appre-

16

ciable period of time. Similarly, the reading one does in waiting rooms or the reading of books borrowed from children's libraries goes by unnoticed. Who will ever be able to completely appreciate the enormous importance of such a book as the *Sapeur Camembert* or *Tintin* in the reading of a cultivated French adult?

The task of analyzing reading habits seems easier when one uses historical evidence. Documents are less embarrassing than personal testimony. Evidence from memoirs, letters, reported conversations, allusions and catalogues of private libraries allows us to reconstruct with a fair degree of certainty the *Belesenheit*, that is, all the reading done by a given person, if he belongs to a rather high social milieu. However, there are virtually no ways of assessing the importance in the cultural behavior of the masses of very numerous reading opportunities available to the public at large. These appeared with the printing press and with hawkers: Charles Nisard has analyzed the influence of hawking in his book on the nineteenth century, *Histoire des livres populaires ou de la littérature de colportage.*[7]

The literary historian must not fail to explore this vast domain. It is what we sometimes call "sub-literature" or "infra-literature," or even sometimes "marginal literature."[8] Between this domain, ignored in textbooks until recent times, and that of "noble" works, constant changes occur in themes, ideas and forms. It sometimes happens that a work moves from one level to the other. In fact, as we shall see, classification as literature or as sub-literature is not a function of the abstract qualities of either the writer, the work, or the public, but is defined through a kind of interchange.[9] The difference, therefore, between what one reads and what one should read, often remarked in past centuries, has always

---

7. See also P. Brochon, *Le Livre de colportage en France depuis le XVIe siècle* (Paris, 1954) and J.-P. Seguin, *Nouvelles à sensations et canards du XIXe siècle* (Paris, 1959).

8. *Littérature et sous-littérature, Bulletin du Séminaire de Littérature générale* (Bordeaux, 1961-2-3), No. X. A. Thérive uses the expression "infra-literature" in his book *La foire littéraire* (Paris, 1963). Finally, Volume III, *L'histoire de la littérature* in the *Encyclopédie de la Pléiade* devotes several chapters to "marginal literatures" (pedlar's literature, the popular novel, etc.). The Sixth Congress of the French Society of Comparative Literature (Rennes, 1963) tackled this problem. See my article, "Y a-t-il des degrés dans la littérature?"

9. Cf. Chapters VI and VIII.

been considered a subject of disgrace by men of letters. It is these men whose evidence is used by the historian and whose work concerns the sociologist.

If we wish, however, to challenge the reader's statements and to question the writer, we will probably be even more discouraged. Writers may shed light on the mechanisms of literary creation, on psychological or material considerations, but not on the author-public interchange. As the act of literary creation is a solitary and free act, it requires a certain detachment from social demands. In other words, if the writer as man and as artist must picture his public for himself and feel himself identified with it, he discovers that too clear an idea of the biases with which his public views him is dangerous to him. The act of literary creation has been compared with that of the castaway who throws a bottle into the sea, and the comparison is fairly exact if we bear in mind that the castaway imagines the rescuer to whom he sends his message, feels himself dependent on him, but does not really know to what distant shores the sea will carry his appeal.

Observations made by middlemen in the book trade could have greater value for us, for publishers, book stores and librarians control the main cogs of the exchange mechanism between author and public. Unfortunately, the first two categories lock away their commercial secrets. Besides, even if publishers and bookstores were willing to give information, they would often be incapable of doing so, for they lack relevant techniques to determine the limits of their function. For most of them, their offices or stores are simply headquarters from which they blindly exercise real and decisive influence on writers and the public.

The librarian's situation is somewhat different, for he is generally able to observe directly the behavior of his readers. But his observations concern only a rather small and special part of his public, that is, the reader in the library. This narrow door must not be ignored, however, as it is practically the only one which opens onto the reality of literary consumption. Study of libraries in business enterprises is the only responsible way of approaching the problem of reading in the working-class environment.

It is only through the study of objective data, systematically exploited without preconceived ideas, that we may approach the literary fact.

Among objective data, the first to be used are statistical in nature. As rare and incomplete as they may be, statistics concerning the book industry can be usefully brought together and can furnish pertinent information. UNESCO is continually adding new statistics to its *Index Translationum*, in the *Cahiers du Centre de Documention*. In France, a corner of the curtain is being raised and various praiseworthy efforts are being made. Such works as the *Monographie de l'Edition*, which we have already mentioned, and better still, lists of best-selling first editions are regularly being published by the *Nouvelles Littéraires*.[10] In addition, many libraries can provide very precise information about readers who frequent their establishments and the books they borrow. Even public polls of this nature can be envisioned.

To the extent that information is accessible, it is equally possible to make use of historical statistics based on lists of works or of writers. These statistics undoubtedly shed light on diverse phenomena of literary evolution. For example, the application of data from a sampling of 937 French writers born between 1490 and 1900 can be found in Figure III.[11]

Statistical data help us to demonstrate the general outlines of the literary fact. Then they must be interpreted through another type of statistical data garnered from the study of social structures; these data frame the literary fact and the technical facts which condition it: political regimes, cultural institutions, classes, social categories and levels, jobs, use of leisure time, degrees of illiteracy, the economic and legal status of the writer the bookseller and the publisher, linguistic problems, the history of books, etc.

Finally, we can initiate the study of specific cases using the methods of general or comparative literature: the vicissitudes of a work, the history of a myth, the evolution of a genre or style, the influence of environment, etc. Then statistical data will demonstrate their value; the researcher, assisted by polls, questionnaires and oral or written evidence, and properly shuffling the information which case histories have given him, can assign all of their significance to objectively observed phenomena.

---

10. For more details, see G. Chaernsol's article in *Informations sociales* (January 1957), pp. 36-48.
11. All the statistical research used in this work was made possible by the technical services of the *Institut National de la Statistique de Bordeaux*.

PART TWO

Production

CHAPTER III

The Writer in Time

Tels qu'en eux-mêmes . . .

LITERARY PRODUCTION is the manifestation of a community of writers which, through the ages, has been submitted to fluctuations analagous to those of all other demographic groups — aging, rejuvenation, overpopulation and decreasing population.

To obtain a definition, or at least a significant sample of this community, two extreme procedures may be envisaged. The first would be to list all authors of published books (however produced) in a country between two given dates. The second would be to refer to an accepted literary history of established quality.

Neither of these procedures, however, is satisfactory. The first is subject to a mechanical definition of what a writer is; i.e., a man who has written a book. Now, we have seen that a mechanical definition of the book is not acceptable, for it fails to account for the convergence or compatibility of intention between reader and author. Similarly, the writer considered as a simple manufacturer of literary products has no literary significance. He only acquires this significance; he may be defined as a writer only in retrospect by an observer from the general public who is capable of perceiving him as such. A writer exists only in relation to at least one other person.

An accepted literary index would appear to be more reliable. But once we examine the index of a literary history we see that, taking the growth of the literary population into account, the number of writers to which it refers increases proportionally as one approaches the date in which the history was written. The evolution is at first very slow, almost negligible, until the names of writers who are contemporaries of the literary historian appear— that is, those writers who were still alive at the time the author of the literary history began his study. In Lanson's literary history, for example, the disparity begins with the Romantics. From that date on, the criterion of choice is less and less demanding. A second disparity occurs if the author is imprudent enough to include his contemporaries in the history (in Lanson, the Symbolists). As a result, either the last pages of the history resemble the mechanical catalogues we wish to avoid or the choice made is perfectly arbitrary and subjective. The choice may not resemble that made by a historian one or two generations later.

Consequently, the image of a community of writers may only be obtained from fixed perspectives. Euripides said that we cannot claim that a man is happy until after his death: in the same way, it is only after a writer's death that he may be defined as a member of the literary collectivity.

Historical perspective allows the historian to examine the community of writers in both a quantitative and qualitative fashion.

Quantitatively, the most decisive and rigorous sorting occurs in the first generation after the writer's lifetime: each writer has a rendezvous with oblivion in the ten, twenty or thirty years after his death. If a writer manages to cross this redoubtable threshold, he becomes integrated with the literary class and is assured of almost permanent survival— at least as long as the collective memory of the civilization which saw him born endures. The resistance of writers to this historical "erosion" is variable; there are weak zones in which few survive (the beginning of the eighteenth century in France, for example) and firmly established groups which better resist the test of time (the second half of the seventeenth century in France).

Other sortings take place later. Spectacular rejuvenations occur, reviving a writer forgotten or neglected for many years; but usually he was not completely forgotten and this phenomenon results from shift of emphasis rather than rediscovery. The revival of Shakespeare in eighteenth-century England is an example. The general conformation of the community of writers is not significantly affected by adjustments which are peculiarly qualitative.

In fact, these shifts of emphasis within an already defined collectivity are of an interpretative nature. Very often they are obtained by discarding the author's original intentions, which have become unintelligible, and substituting new, surmised intentions compatible with the needs of a new public. This mechanism will here be called "creative treason."

The qualitative effects of historical perspective have been brought to light by Harvey C. Lehman, the American psychologist who developed a particularly ingenious method.[1] Lehman used a list of the "most important" books, a list established after consultation with the National Council of Teachers of English. The list included 337 works by 203 authors already dead at the time it was compiled and 396 works by 285 living authors. Lehman first established the age of each author at the time he wrote the works on the list. Then, the works of living authors and the works of deceased authors were classified according to the writer's age: books written between 20-25, between 25-30, etc. He then projected on a graph the data for both groups. The difference between the two curves is remarkable. The one marking deceased authors rapidly attained its apex between 35-40 years and then descended. The other curve climbed more slowly, reaching its apex between 40-45 years, but then remained at a rather high level until 70-75. The conclusion is obvious: the selection made through historical perspective affects mature works and especially works created in old age which are eliminated in favor of works created in youth. The mean critical age occurs at about 40.

This result may be verified by other procedures. One should always remember that the quality through which the writer will survive in the community of writers, "tel qu'en

---

1. "The Creative Years: Best Books," *The Scientific Monthly* (July 1937), VL, 65-75.

2. This is approximately the first line of Mallarmé's sonnet, "Le Tombeau D'Edgar Poe." The exact line is *"Tel qu'en Lui-même enfin l'éternité le change."* [Translator's note]

lui-même enfin l'éternité le change,"[2] is approximately that which was striking when he was about 40.[3]

The sampling of a literary community must take these various factors into account. It is a long and delicate job. For most of his statistics, Lehman used "best book" lists compiled by Asa Don Dickinson, former librarian of the University of California. Dickinson's selective process consisted of comparing lists of diverse types, classifying works into Grade 1, Grade 2, etc.

In a more modest and less systematic fashion, the procedure used in this study was analagous to that of Lehman. It was used to establish a list of 937 French writers born beween 1490 and 1900, on which most of the following observations were based.

The goal was to give the sampling as extensive a sociological base as possible. Therefore, it would have been unwise to make use of the index of a literary history, as previously suggested, even for dead writers. It would have included only the type of "cultured" writer. In fact, literary phenomena move in a given society in closed circuits and often without intercommunication. A writing community corresponds to the "cultured" public; this community is the one we know best and which is revealed to us through literary histories; but, as we shall see, it represents only a small part of the real community. Maurice Leblanc, father of Arsène Lupin and a member of the "popular" group, and Beatrix Potter, celebrant of little rabbits and a member of the "juvenile" group, are hardly ever mentioned in literary textbooks. However, they have had and still have a considerable audience and they are at the basis of incontestable literary facts.

Thus it is preferable to use as basic documents lists of an encyclopedic nature (*Petit-Larousse, Dictionary of National Biography*) rather than textbooks, and then collate them with specialized lists of different origins (*Dictionnaire des Oeuvres*, publishing house catalogues, translations, bibliographies, periodic indices, etc.). In this way, one obtains a sample possessing real sociological significance.

3.. This is only a statistical indication and it is easy to find exceptions. We have examined the exact meaning of the age factor in an article originally published in the *Bulletin des Bibliothèques de France* (May 1960), entitled: "Le facteur âge dans la productivité littéraire." [See Appendix for a translation of this article.]

All samples may be challenged in their details, but experience proves that, if necessary precautions have been taken, a normal distribution can be obtained by this method. The general aspect of this distribution scarcely changes if the elements of choice or the severity of criteria are modified.

Generations and "Teams"

The first phenomenon which permits the study of such a sample is that of "generations." Generations, as they have been understood by Albert Thibaudet or Henri Peyre, are obvious phenomena: in each literature, the dates of authors' births may be grouped together in chronological periods. A complete list of generations, valid for several European literatures, will be found in the work of Henri Peyre.[4]

For example, the great Romantic generation in France around 1800, which succeeded a generation of relatively poor writers, gave birth between 1795 and 1805 to such men as Augustin Thierry, Michelet, August Comte, Balzac, Hugo, Lacordaire, Mérimée, Dumas, Quinet, Sainte-Beuve, George Sand, Eugène Sue, Blanqui and Eugénie de Guérin. Other great generations are those of Spain in 1585, of France in 1600-1610, of England in 1675-1685, etc.

The idea of generations must, however, be approached with a good deal of circumspection. The first trap to avoid is that of the "temptation of cycles." It is rather pleasant to imagine that these chronological groups follow one another at regular intervals. When Henri Peyre speaks of the "alternating rhythm of generations," he is alluding to an infinitely complex mechanism which we shall analyze later, but this rhythm is not regular by any means. Guy Michaud, who is bolder (or less prudent), sees a sinusoidal and even helicoidal rhythm in the succession of generations; each rhythmic period corresponds to the span of human life, about 70 years.[5] In spite of the attraction of such an hypothesis and our real attempt to verify its accuracy, in this study we have never been able to perceive regular, unquestionable rhythms in the generation theory. However, to be more precise, it is neces-

---

4. "Tableau récapitulatif des générations," *Les générations littéraires*, pp. 214-217.
5. *Introduction à une science de la littérature,* pp. 252-256 and p. 258. See also the chart on p. 259 which explains literary movements by the regular alternation of generations. For Guy Michaud, the human "day" of 72 years is divided into four half-generations of 18 years each, the first two of which are "nocturnal" (death and flux), while the latter are "diurnal" (plenitude and reflux).

sary to add that certain literary phenomena recur from time to time in periodic modifications which would support in part the 70-year theory.

For example the "life" of a literary genre— Elizabethan tragedy, classical tragedy, the realistic English novel of the eighteenth century, romantic forms— is generally from thirty to thirty-five years, or half a lifetime. An experiment, which unfortunately we cannot chart graphically here, appears to corroborate this observation. We superimposed curves, each representing in our sampling the respective number of novelists, poets, playwrights and other writers, composing the whole literary population (the polygraphs each counting several times). It is clear that the chart changes radically every 70 years and partially every 35 years, as one genre dominates the others or diminishes. It is, however, difficult to establish the slightest relation between this apparently constant rhythm and that of "generations of writers."

As a second observation, literary generations differ from biological generations in that they constitute numerically identifiable groups. Within the general population of a country, the distribution of age groups varies slowly and within relatively narrow limits. Age distribution in a general population differs from the ideal "bell" curve in a certain number

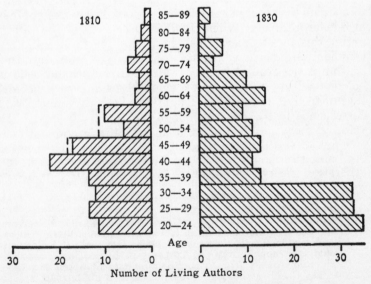

Fig. 1: French Literature: Age Distribution 1810-1830

of characteristic details which are interpreted by the demographer but which nevertheless remain largely faithful to that form. On the contrary, age distribution in a literary population, because of dramatic enlargements and reductions, cannot be reduced to an ideal type. (See Figure I)

A systematic study of age distributions through the centuries leads us to believe that a generation of writers does not make its appearance until the bulk of the preceding generation is more than forty years old. It is as if we were dealing with a balance; writers only yield their places due to the weight of new writers.

A third observation ensues from the preceding one. When we speak of a generation of writers, the significant date can be neither the date of a writer's birth nor the date of his majority. We are not born writers, we become them, and it is exceedingly rare to be an author at the age of twenty. Accession to literary status is a complex process; the decisive period is reached somewhere around the age of forty, but this is extremely variable. We must think in terms of "age zones" rather than of precise age. Thus, Richardson (born in 1689) came late to literature yet is the biological contemporary of Pope (born in 1688); generally, he is attached to the generation of Fielding (born in 1707). Frequently

---

Figure 1 shows two examples of age distribution in the French literary population. These two pyramids are separated by twenty years. In the first, which shows the situation in 1810, the great philosophers have disappeared; they would have been between 90 and 100 years old. One can still distinguish, however, from 70 to 80 years, the generation of Beaumarchais and Bernardin de Saint-Pierre of which l'Abbé Delille is one of the last survivors. After a ten year interval it is followed by a powerful generation which will last twenty years; it includes Rivarol (57 years old), Madame de Staël (44), and Chateaubriand (42). This is Napoleon's generation: the guillotine destroys much of it and thus causes the dotted lines; but still bursting with life, this generation dominates the world of letters. The following generation seems only its shadow; great names become rare but occasionally occur: Nodier (30), Béranger (30), Lamennais (28) and Stendhal (27). In 1830, everything changes: the great generation of the Revolution and the Empire has wasted away and leaves the field to young talents. Lamartine reaches forty, Vigny and Balzac have just passed thirty and Hugo is almost thirty; Musset is twenty years old. This flowering will last for five years— long enough to give us Gautier— then the literary scene, once more saturated, will once again become dormant until the generation of Flaubert and Baudelaire.

27

young generations include a "pilot" in their midst who is older than the rest: in differing degrees, Goethe, Nodier and Carlyle are pilots.

The idea of generations, at first attractive, is not absolutely faultless. Perhaps it would be better to substitute the word "group," a word which is much more supple and organic. A "group" is the team of writers of any given age which "speaks," or occupies the literary scene during a particular epoch. Consciously or not, it blocks entrance to that scene for a certain time, forbidding new talents to emerge.

What events provoke these groups or permit them to form and to take over the literary scene? It seems that they are political events which, in turn, involve a change of personnel— changes of reigns, revolutions, wars, etc.

An extremely suggestive graph will be found in Figure II. It indicates the proportion of writers from 20 to 40 years old for the last three centuries in France. When the curve climbs, it shows that the literary population is becoming more youthful; when it descends, it shows fewer recruits or an aging literary group. The lowest points show a "departure," the accession of a new group, and correspond to peaceful times (the end of the religious wars in 1598, the end of the Fronde in 1652) and to the last years of a reign (Louis XIV, Louis XV, Napoleon I, Napoleon III). The highest points indicate "blockades" which correspond to rigid political regimes: that of Richelieu (symbolized by the Academy), that of Louis XV, that of the Revolutionary government, the latter confirmed and aggravated by the newly academic nature of the First Empire. One can even distinguish the arresting influence of the "moral order" on the generation that was coming of age following the displacement of the Second Empire.

In David T. Pottinger's book, *The French Book Trade in the Ancient Regime*, figures are made available with which to calculate the "productive curve" of French writers between 1550 and 1800. It corresponds to the age curve but with a lag of twenty years.[6]

Applied to English literature, the same method produces identical results. Two great periods of "aging" are to be observed: during the reign of Queen Elizabeth I from 1599 (the Armada) to 1625 (the death of James I) and during the reign of Queen Victoria from 1837 to 1877.

We may regret the lack of a regular rhythm or measurable periodicity in these curves. It would be undoubtedly satifying to observe literary facts regulated to fit a mechanical and mathematical rhythm, but is it not more revealing to notice their relationship to society? The nature of that relationship remains to be defined.

6. See Appendix.

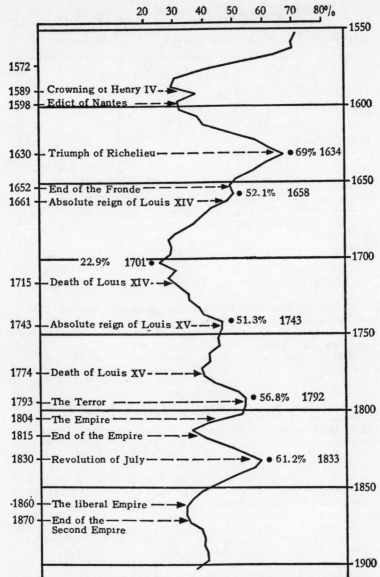

Fig. 2: French Literature: curve of writers less than forty years old who were producing from 1550-1900. The figures used here are derived from annual percentages which have been averaged over five year periods. The points outside of the curve indicate exact percentages for the maximum and the minimum years.

Addendum

Curves of literary genres in relation to the total of living authors.

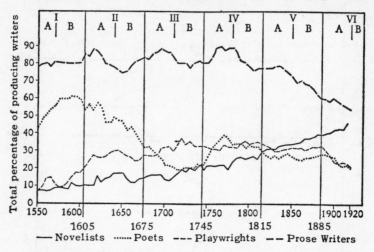

— Novelists   ······· Poets   --- Playwrights   — — Prose Writers

The graph above, resulting from an experiment, seems to confirm observations we made in Chapter III of *Sociology of Literature*. In our selected model, we have superimposed curves which represent the percentages of novelists, poets, playwrights and other prose writers of the total of these literary groups. At first, one sees that the prose-writer curve, which is highest, is represented in half-periods of thirty-five years in an almost wavelike curve. Because of this periodic repetition, the graph is divided by six chronological eras which are subdivided into categories A and B. One finds, in intervals of about 70 years, five key dates: 1605, 1675, 1745, 1815 and 1885. Their meaning for literary history is not quite clear, even were it possible to find any relation among them. If we look at the theatre, poetry and novel curves, then we see that these other genres have their own key dates.

In the first period, the one that corresponds to the last three-fourths of the sixteenth century, poetry is at its peak. In the second period, that of the "Baroque," poetry stays near its peak but begins a steep decline while the theatre gains and assumes a position between poetry and the novel. In the third period, the age of Classicism, poetry falls to its nadir while the theatre reaches its zenith and assumes a position of supremacy. Simultaneously, while the novel begins to rise, it meets but does not surpass poetry in 1745. In the fourth period, while "sentimentality" grew with the Romantic crisis, poetry began a counteroffensive which was abruptly halted in the middle of the period. During the Revolution, the theatre rose once more to its previous high point. The relation of theatre to poetry around 1815 was approximately the same as around 1745. In the fifth period, parallel to the years in which Victor Hugo wrote, the novel jumped to a position between the theatre and poetry. The beginning of a marked decline in the prose writers' curve becomes obvious. In the sixth period, which ends in 1955, the novel increased markedly and began to approach prose while the other forms of literature continued to diminish.

30

Years	Novelists	Poets	Playwrights	Prose Writers
1550	7.0	43.5	7.0	78.2
1555	7.2	48.0	9.7	79.6
1560	7.1	50.4	14.2	80.0
1565	7.3	53.6	14.6	78.0
1570	8.6	55.5	11.1	81.1
1575	8.9	59.3	8.9	80.8
1580	8.7	59.8	9.6	80.3
1585	8.0	59.9	11.7	80.1
1590	11.5	61.0	15.0	80.0
1595	10.0	60.8	17.5	79.8
1600	9.9	59.4	17.3	81.1
1605	10.1	53.8	20.3	85.2
1610	10.2	56.2	24.3	84.3
1615	10.1	53.6	27.6	88.7
1620	15.1	57.5	26.7	87.4
1625	12.1	54.7	26.8	84.3
1630	14.1	46.6	27.0	80.0
1635	15.0	46.5	29.0	79.0
1640	17.2	49.6	30.2	78.0
1645	17.3	47.8	30.5	75.9
1650	17.7	46.7	29.3	74.7
1655	14.7	42.1	27.5	75.4
1660	12.6	43.8	26.5	78.4
1665	12.1	40.6	24.4	80.3
1670	13.9	36.8	24.9	81.7
1675	14.7	32.7	27.9	83.8
1680	15.8	32.8	27.8	82.5
1685	16.7	30.7	27.6	85.4
1690	16.5	28.9	28.1	86.7
1695	16.4	25.6	31.4	88.5
1700	13.8	22.6	32.1	87.7
1705	13.2	22.1	32.8	86.5
1710	15.0	20.3	30.3	83.4
1715	17.5	19.9	33.7	80.3
1720	19.6	19.6	37.4	80.2
1725	18.6	20.4	34.1	80.6
1730	20.2	20.6	35.8	78.0
1735	19.7	20.8	33.3	80.5
1740	21.1	22.5	33.7	81.5
1745	22.3	21.7	33.6	80.9
1750	19.4	26.3	32.9	80.8

Years	Novelists	Poets	Playwrights	Prose Writers
1755	21.9	31.3	31.5	83.5
1760	22.1	34.3	31.5	88.3
1765	21.8	36.7	30.8	89.8
1770	22.1	39.1	33.8	88.1
1775	22.1	36.7	32.7	89.0
1780	19.8	33.1	32.5	89.4
1785	23.9	34.1	32.2	86.7
1790	25.9	34.9	34.6	82.0
1795	26.4	33.0	35.8	80.8
1800	25.7	33.5	34.5	78.8
1805	26.2	32.7	34.9	76.1
1810	26.8	32.4	35.2	77.4
1815	25.7	29.9	34.2	77.3
1820	29.0	27.4	33.2	77.9
1825	31.1	26.6	32.1	77.9
1830	31.2	27.5	30.6	78.7
1835	31.1	26.7	30.6	79.0
1840	33.1	27.5	31.1	77.7
1845	33.4	28.5	31.8	75.5
1850	34.1	27.3	32.6	73.3
1855	34.1	26.0	32.0	69.9
1860	34.7	25.7	32.0	70.5
1865	35.2	26.7	31.0	69.0
1870	37.0	26.1	31.7	68.2
1875	37.3	27.2	32.6	66.2
1880	38.0	27.6	32.8	62.5
1885	39.9	28.8	33.2	60.6
1890	39.8	28.6	30.6	60.2
1895	40.1	27.5	27.6	59.3
1900	41.2	26.3	24.2	60.5
1905	42.2	23.4	23.5	58.8
1910	43.3	22.2	24.2	56.7
1915	43.1	22.7	23.4	55.9
1920	46.9	21.8	21.5	54.7

CHAPTER IV

The Writer in Society

The Origins

IN ORDER to fix a writer's place in society, the first step is to investigate his origins. Most biographers take that precaution in individual cases, but we are less enlightened as to the collective traits of those origins. A precursor in this field was Henry Havelock Ellis, who, at the end of the last century, applied a statistical method to what he termed the analysis of genius.[1] From his research let us retain two principal preoccupations: research into geographical origins and research into socio-professional origins.

Literary geography has become a fad within the last few years.[2] Perhaps we should not demand much from it: from geography one quickly abstracts to regionalism and from regionalism to racism. We have been content up to this point to make use of the crude data of the place of birth. That alone suffices to shed light on a certain number of phenomena which we shall now expound.

It leads, in particular, to the study of the fascinating problem of the Paris-province balance in France. There is not room here to reproduce graphs fully to illustrate that balance, but this information will suffice: 31 per cent of the 937 writers we considered were born in Paris— and the proportion of Parisians in ratio to all writers in France was particularly great between 1630 and 1720, having a culminating point of 50.2 per cent between 1665 and 1669. The eighteenth century, in contrast, is predominantly provincial, especially between 1740 and 1744 (28.1%). In the nineteenth century, the phenomenon of "national distribution" which we shall study later on, maintains a proportion of 35.9 per cent

---

1. *A Study of British Genius* (London, 1904). See the passage that Henri Peyre devotes to him in his *Les générations littéraires*, pp. 80-81.

2. A. Dupouy, *Géographie des lettres françaises* (Paris, 1942), and A. Ferré, *Géographie littéraire* (Paris, 1946).

between 1860 and 1864. These fragmentary statistics confirm the frequently expressed ideas of our colleague, Pierre Barrière, on the Paris-province alternation. Figure III represents the distribution of the number of writers born in six different periods. For the period 1490-1580 (from Rabelais to Mathurin Regnier), the Royal Domain dominates all others: Normandy, Champagne, the Loire Valley, Aunis and Saintonge, and Périgord. The period 1580-1650 (from Racan to La Bruyère) is above all represented by the Paris and Rouen regions (Corneille, for example). Most writers of the period 1650-1720 (from Fénelon to D'Alembert) were, however, born in the provinces: Brittany at the beginning of the period, then Languedoc, and finally other provincial centers appeared. In addition to Rouen there were now Tours, Grenoble and especially Dijon, whose academy was vigorously active. Between 1720 and 1790 (from Marmontel to Lamartine), the movement to the provinces is once more notable. Before the Revolution, those areas indicated by dense zones in Figure III were grouped around the seats of Parliament, but soon, with the advent of the Revolution, regions appear which were relatively unimportant before this time. This is the beginning of "distribution": with rare exceptions almost all of France is productive between 1790 and 1860 (from Scribe to Jules Laforgue). The maps in Figure III indicate that the most populous zones are Marseilles, Bordeaux, Lyons and Lille. A final map, more subject to caution than the others, sketches what is the distribution for the forty years between 1860 and 1900 (from Barrès to Saint-Exupéry): urban concentration is confirmed (Toulouse, Nice, Besançon, Nancy and Caen enter into the picture) and perhaps now the influence of the universities is distinguishable.

It is with great caution that we indicate the possible influence of milieux and institutions— classes, academies, urban centers, universities— on literary vocations. Any research which seeks to elucidate these phenomena will have to be undertaken with extreme care. Analysis and criticism will have to evolve further before we can claim results on which to base research of the phenomena mentioned above. Notably, such variables as moving from one region to another and accidental vocations must be taken into account.

We will have to establish a set of statistics on socioprofessional origins on which only fragmentary and unsatisfactory work has been done; this information is difficult to obtain. Two incomplete polls deal with certain French and English writers of the nineteenth century and demonstrate what we may hope from further research.

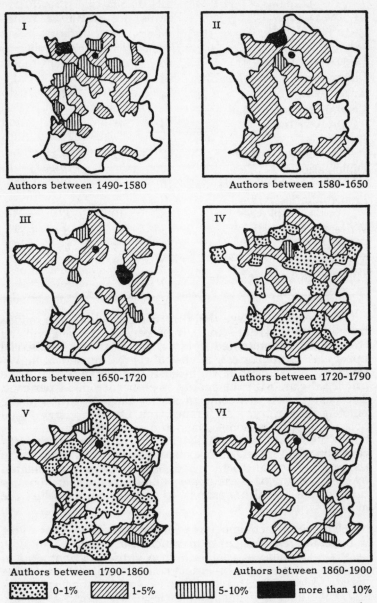

Authors between 1490-1580

Authors between 1580-1650

Authors between 1650-1720

Authors between 1720-1790

Authors between 1790-1860

Authors between 1860-1900

0-1%   1-5%   5-10%   more than 10%

Fig. 3: The percentages refer to all writers in France born during the periods we are considering. The territorial divisions which we have used as a base are present departments whose boundaries often coincide with former provinces.

Categories	ENGLAND		FRANCE	
	Parents %	Writers %	Parents %	Writers %
Leisure aristocracy	18	2	8	9
Clergy	14	4	—	4
Army, Navy	4	4	24	4
Liberal professions, universities	14	12	16	8
Industries, businesses, banks	12	2	20	0
Diplomatic, administrative posts	10	8	4	16
Lesser administrative posts, employees	8	10	8	8
Writers and artists	8	44	8	52
Politicians	2	4	4	8
Technicians	2	2	0	0
Manual workers, peasants	8	0	8	0

For each country, the first column shows the milieu favorable to a writer's incubation period. In England, an entire zone is represented from the gentry to the commercial upper class; nevertheless, in view of its real numerical importance in the country, it is obviously the clergy which is the privileged class with the enormous proportion of 14 per cent. The pastor's son was common among English writers of the nineteenth century. In France, the Catholic clergy could not— and with reason— claim the same distinction. This fell to the Army: to the minister's son corresponded the officer's son (in general, of Napoleon's army). In addition to the army,— the aristocracy had been just about annihilated by the Revolution,— the upper middle class of merchants or those of the liberal professions, as in England, furnished the mass of writers.

The second column gives information of another type; it indicates the categories to which the writers themselves belong. One notices that in both countries (44 per cent in England, 52 per cent in France), about half belong to the "arts and letters" category. That is, socially and professionally, they earn a living from their artistic work; these are "men of letters." However, scarcely eight per cent came from this same milieu. On the other hand, thirty-two per cent of the writers of both countries either are involved in liberal professions (most are in universities), or are of the higher or lesser administration. These proportions were the same for their parents (32 per cent in England, 28 per cent in France). This proves that these categories, as opposed to the others mentioned here, are compatible with the practice of literary activities. We can only conclude that from one generation to the other, a concentration occurs around a middle zone of the social scale which constitutes what we shall call the "literary milieu."[3]

This phenomenon of the "literary milieu" is characteristic of the nineteenth and twentieth centuries. It did not always exist.[4] For this reason we must now examine the evolution of economic relations between writer and society; in other words, the writer's métier.

The Problem of Finances

To understand the nature of a writer's work, it must be remembered that even the most ethereal of poets eats and sleeps each day. Thus, each literary fact raises the problem of financing, without collateral, the writer as a man, apart from the problem of financing the publication, which we shall discuss later.

The problem is as old as the world: it is proverbial to say that literature does not feed its creator. Conversely, it would be senseless to deny the influence that material considerations have had on literary output. The potboiler is not

---

3. Compare our percentages with statistics published by *L'Express,* November 27, 1954, dealing with 128 novels published in 1954:
   41% by "men of letters"
   16% by professors
   10% by lawyers
   7% by civil servants
   5% by engineers
   2% by doctors

   It is necessary to add a "sundry" category, of which 4% are manual laborers. These statistics are similar to ours and show that if a change has taken place, it is in favor of the liberal professions and, particularly, of the University group.

4. In his book, *The French Book Trade in the Ancient Regime,* David T. Pottinger gives figures which allow us to establish a picture of the family environment of French writers in the sixteenth, seventeenth and eighteenth centuries. The absence of a "literary milieu" is to be noted:

Noblesse d'épée - - - - -	28 %
Noblesse de robe et de clocher -	31 %
Clergy - - - - - -	6 %
Third Estate - - - -	66 %
Upper middle class - - -	20.5%
Middle class - - - - -	4.5%
Craftsmen and peasants - -	10 %

   [Those members of the *noblesse d'épée* category were descendants of the old feudal nobility. Those of the *nobless de robe et de clocher* category were descendants of the middle class. They became the new aristocracy because of their inherited status and landed property. For the most part they were wealthy judges.]

37

always bad. It was, we are told, the need of money which induced Cervantes to write novels and consequently, *Don Quixote*. The desire to bolster his wavering financial condition made a novelist out of Walter Scott, the poet. As for the literary dearth in the English theatre during the first part of the nineteenth century, lack of adequate royalties may reasonably explain that situation.[5]

Some years ago, a series, whose success was unfortunately not as great as its merits, raised this question about a certain number of great writers: "What Did They Live On?" Numerous and provocative indications may be found in that series.[6] This research must once more be renewed and continued in a systematic fashion.

Basically, there are but two ways a writer can make his living: internal financing through royalties, of which we shall have more to say later on, and external financing. The latter boils down to two types: patronage and self-financing.

Patronage is the support of a writer by a person or an institution that protects him but that, in return, expects satisfaction of the cultural need. The relations between client and patron are not without parallels in history: i.e., the liege-suzerain relationship. The patron, like a feudal organization, corresponds to a social structure founded on autonomous units. The absence of a common literary milieu (lack of culture or absence of the middle classes), the lack of a profitable distribution method, the concentration of money in the hands of the few, the intellectual refinement of the aristocracy, made necessary the appearance of closed systems. In such a system, the writer was considered an artisan, a purveyor of luxury items, and his output was bartered to assure his upkeep.

The *Familia* of the rich imperial Roman undoubtedly represents the social structure best adapted to patronage. It owes its name to the famous Maecenus, friend of Augustus and protector of Horace. But patronage was especially developed in royal and even Papal courts. The patron only yielded his place when wealth became more evenly distributed, when more and more levels of society immersed themselves in intellectual activities, and when profitable methods of distribution, such as the printing press, were invented. The institution of patronage exists even now in the form of government or at least public support.

---

5. Until the Copyright Act of 1842, English playwrights were practically at the mercy of theatrical directors and actors. On this subject, see the revealing conversation between Walter Scott and Lord Byron quoted in R. Escarpit's *Lord Byron, un tempérament littéraire* (Paris, 1957), II, 154-155.

6. Published by *Les Editions des Deux-Rives*, this series included R. Bouvier's and E. Maynal's *Balzac*, J. Rousselot's *Verlaine*, J. L. Loiselet's *Molière* and J. Donvez's *Voltaire*.

Throughout the ages, governmental patronage has been expressed by grants of more or less regular pensions or by the bestowal of official titles, such as *Poet Laureate* in England or *King's Historian* in France. Bureaucratic sinecures may be considered a form of governmental patronage and several French writers of the nineteenth century owed their living to them.

The existence of indirect patronage should also be mentioned. By influencing the literary market, indirect patronage can procure revenues for authors which otherwise might not be anticipated. For example, a government can order great quantities of a book for its public libraries and its information services. The most common method, however, is that of the literary prize, which has the advantage of being quite economical. The monetary value of such a prize is generally nominal, but it assures the winner considerable sales and, consequently, revenue. However, certain prizes, such as the Nobel Prize for Literature, represent large endowments.

It is difficult to criticize patronage. To scorn this practice in its traditional form (or in its present form of prize-giving) is to demonstrate a ridiculous kind of Pharisaism. Besides the fact that patronage has had the merit of making possible the integration of the writer into the economic cycle to which he previously did not belong (and thus permitting him to exist and produce), an often happy influence on letters must be credited to it. If Louis XIV's patronage of Molière had not set him relatively free from the paying public, we would have had more plays like *La Princesse d'Elide* than like *Dom Juan*.

The Egyptian writer, Taha Hussein, has given the problem its true economic significance: "This is dishonest traffic: the patron gives gold or silver which is spent by the man of letters as he receives it; the writer gives his art or his thought, neither of which can be spent under any circumstances."[7]

In other words, although it has been of service, patronage no longer fulfills the demands of our social morality and can no longer be considered as a normal and healthy institution in our time. To replace it, Taha Hussein thinks that moonlighting is the least reprehensible solution. And this solution is hardly new:

Aristotle was Alexander's teacher, Pliny the Younger was a high functionary in the Roman Empire, Bacon a statesman in England, Chateaubriand a French ambassador then a minister, Mallarmé a teacher,

---

7. "L'écrivain dans la société moderne," was a lecture presented at the International Conference of Artists (Venice, 1952), and published in *L'artiste dans la société contemporaine*, U.N.E.S.C.O. (1954), pp. 72-87.

Giraudoux a diplomat. How many writers were monks, magistrates, or doctors? Some like Cervantes and Agrippa d'Aubigné were even soldiers.[8]

In fact, moonlighting is but a form of self-financing. We can even speak of auto-patronage when one's financial needs are assured by personal wealth, but this has become more and more rare. Byron was one of the last authors who wanted to be a "gentleman who writes," and he had to give it up. But how many Bohemian poets have been financed by money inherited from less poetic ancestors! Verlaine is a notable example.[9]

On the other hand, one thinks of Voltaire, whose extraordinary range of remunerative activities permitted him to live and to get rich. One may find the whole scale of financial resources, including pensions granted by patrons, his profits as an editor, his royalties, but especially the skilful speculation, the commercial ingenuity that he demonstrated as a clockmaking industrialist and the vigilance of the money-grubbing land-owner.[10]

The statistics given above and Taha Hussein's list are enough to show that the income-producing job belongs to a well-defined type: that of the liberal profession or the administration. It is, in fact, a first job rather than a second one, but a job which, on the one hand, leaves some leisure time and which, on the other, does not demand much of an adaptation to the moral and material conditions requisite to literary creation.

The first and perhaps gravest objection to the necessity of having a second job is that only one socio-professional category includes men who write. It is not without cause that present-day French literature is characterized as a "literature of professors." The effects on literary output are not serious. As Taha Hussein states forcefully, to discover a didactic tone in the work of a teacher or careless haste in the work of a journalist, simply because he is a teacher or journalist is bad critical thinking, the kind that comes from *a priori* judgments. More disturbing is the fact that the literary vocation in a manual laborer or peasant, precisely because of his second job, can be realized only if he changes his social level, and that is practically impossible.

Another objection is a moral one. No profession, even a liberal one, exists without having its own ethical requirements. They are not always compatible with the necessary liberty of the writer. By liberty we mean the freedom of

---

8. *Ibid.*
9. See J. Rousselot's *De quoi vivait Verlaine?*
10. See J. Donvez's *De quoi vivait Voltaire?*

following one's imagination anywhere it may lead, of using all elements of one's experience to re-create reality, of having a private life outside one's profession.

A second job must be considered an acceptable solution, but one limited in its effects. Modern society can assent to it as a successor to patronage, but that does not absolve society from raising and resolving the problem of integrating the "job of letters" into its socio-economic system.

The Business of Letters

If one had to give a symbolic date for the emergence of the man of letters, 1755 might be proposed. This is the date of the famous letter written by Samuel Johnson to Lord Chesterfield refusing his help, although Johnson had vainly solicited this help years earlier at the time he was preparing his dictionary:

> Seven years, my Lord, have now passed, since I waited in your outward rooms, or was repulsed from your door; during which time I have been pushing on in my work through difficulties, of which it is useless to complain, and have brought it, at last, to the verge of publication, without one act of assistance, one word of encouragement, or one smile of favour.[11]

These lines toll the bell for patronage. Johnson succeeded in living— in surviving— by his pen, although it must be admitted that he later accepted a pension. The fact is that he was living at the dawn of a struggle which was to last for two centuries. Since 1709, a law known as Queen Anne's Statute had existed in England, granting rather illusory protections to the writer against the abuses of printers and booksellers. But no legal control was possible until the appearance, towards the middle of the eighteenth century, of commercial entrepreneurs who took responsibility for literary property; that is to say, publishers. It was the French Revolution that spurred this reform.

The protection of an author's royalties consists of guaranteeing his literary property for a period which may vary from twenty-eight years in the United States— and this may be renewed— to perpetuity in Portugal. In France this period covers the author's lifetime plus fifty years, to which may be added certain prolongations stipulated by law. During that period, an author can abandon his royalties through contractual agreement.

What began as national legislation was extended by the Convention of Berne in 1886. This Convention met several

---

11. Letter to Lord Chesterfield, the 7th of February 1755, quoted by Boswell in his *Life of Dr. Johnson*.

times, and in 1956 it included forty-three countries. For their part the Americas, in 1889, had concluded the Convention of Montevideo. In 1952, UNESCO drafted plans for a world convention of royalties, which became effective in 1955 and to which forty countries subscribe, but it is not a substitute for the Berne Convention.

The influence of royalty laws on literary production will be clearly illustrated by the example of American literature at the beginning of the nineteenth century. American publishers were not at that time linked by any pact with English publishers. Thus they were able to reproduce all the works of great contemporary English writers without paying royalties. The situation naturally led them to neglect American authors, whom they would have had to pay. This disastrous competition thus forced American writers to fall back on magazines and on the literary mode best suited to the magazine, the short story. To this fact we partly owe, on the other hand, abundant production of short stories in America in the nineteenth century— notably those of Edgar Allen Poe.[12]

However, if these laws defined the existence and duration of royalties, they did not always regulate the author's enjoyment of them. In the eighteenth and nineteenth centuries, numerous trials set authors against publishers, usually revolving around the problem of "pirate" editions (American or Dutch for the most part).

There are two types of royalty regulations— the outright sale of the author's work or a percentage of sales. With the outright sale of his work, the author receives one lump sum in exchange for which he gives up all his royalties to the publisher, whatever the subsequent success of the work. In percentage payments, the author receives a fraction of the net sale price of each book sold. This fraction may amount from five per cent for scientific works to twelve or fifteen for best sellers. Certain contracts even foresee a progressive percentage, the percentage climbing in direct ratio to the volume of sales. Moreover, the publisher gives the author at certain fixed times (receipt of the manuscript, release of the book, etc.) one or more guaranteed advances on a stipulated number of copies.

Between these two extremes, there exists an infinite variety of possible arrangements. As an example, we will cite Balzac's contract with Hetzel, Paulin, Dubochet and Sauches for the publication of the *Comédie Humaine*. This contract is typical of his era. Balzac was to receive fifty centimes— which was generous— for each of 60,000 volumes (twenty volumes multiplied by editions of 3,000 each), or 30,000

---

12. Fred Lewis Pattee made the comment in his article, "Short Story," in the *Encyclopedia Britannica*.

francs. But if 15,000 francs cash were to be paid at the out-set, as they were, then the 15,000 remaining francs would be paid only after two-thirds of the edition had been sold. This never happened. Furthermore, Balzac had to give back 5,000 of the 15,000 francs to his publisher for corrections. Beyond a certain limit, the author's corrections of galley-proofs are at his own expense . . . and Balzac erased and crossed out abundantly.

The development of radio and television and the conclusion of international agreements have augmented the values of translation and adaptation rights. These rights are normally divided equally between author and publisher. A publishing contract begins increasingly to take on the character of a capital-labor agreement, and many countries feel the necessity of guaranteeing payment to the author through appropriate legislation. However, abuses are still numerous and scandalous outright sale contracts are still frequent. So it would be imprudent to consider the career of letters as an easy way to become rich.

In France, few books attain a world sale of 10,000 copies — less than four per cent of the total. A novelist who manages to sell 20,000 copies of his works each year is an exception. The income corresponding to that amount of sales (after taxes, for royalties are assessed by proportional taxes and progressive surtaxes) is about 800 francs per month (about $160 in 1962). And this occurs only through persistent work (an average of two novels per year) and without financial aid from social legislation. Another example: a young novelist who takes his manuscript to a publisher with the idea of making ten thousand francs from the sale of his work has less chance of making that amount than if he bought the tenth part of a ticket in the National Lottery.

Many kinds of organizations exist in order to protect the rights of authors. One of the most venerable is the *Société des Gens de Lettres*, founded in 1838. It links its efforts with the powerful *Société des Auteurs, Compositeurs, et Editeurs*. In England, the defender of the copyright holder is the *Incorporated Society of Authors, Playwrights and Composers*, founded in 1884. The American equivalent is the Authors' League of America, begun in 1912. Organizations of this kind exist in all countries. Some— Communist countries, of course, but France as well— even have unions for writers. The demands of writers tend more and more towards the establishment of a social charter to protect their rights.

The project of the *Caisse des Lettres* approaches most closely this kind of social charter in France. It has been argued by Parliament and writers for many years. While the *Caisse des Lettres* is far from satisfying the hopes which were placed in it at its inception, its very structure, based on the principle of a kind of mutual social society, has made of it an institution which will be extremely important in the future. It is financed by the government, by publishers and by dues from authors' royalties.

For the moment, the man of letters who does not write best sellers, who has not benefited from a prize or who has not been enriched by movie adaptations of his work, has but a limited choice of solutions should he refuse a second job. The simplest is to take a salaried job, usually as a journalist, or as an employee in a publishing firm, i.e., reader, corrector, literary consultant. There exists also the half-salaried posiion in the stable of writers attached by long term contracts to certain publishers; these writers live on advances. For the rest, a whole gamut of lesser literary work is possible— adaptations, translations, documentary books—which would often gain by being left in the hands of specialists; but unfortunately such experts are rare and demand more stimulating kinds of work. Even beyond these is the vast domain of the alimentary literature of "potboilers," as the English say. That kind of work may have its moments of nobility, especially in the detective novel and the adventure novel; it also has its moments of ugliness. Organized in *factories*, potboilers can provide comfortable incomes to those *managers of literature*, of whom Alexandre Dumas was an example, but who flourish today more than ever. It is here that the proletariat of the pen, slave laborers, find work in writing what others sign or what the merchants of this sub-literature bring out under pink, candy-coated pseudonyms. Nine-tenths of the population satisfy their reading hunger with such novels.

Thus we reach the lowest level of the literary population which is curiously unbalanced because it has not as yet been able to find its social level and, above all, its economic niche in modern civilization. Only a long, analytical study would allow us to define the profound causes of this lack of equilibrium. An examination of the system of distribution will at least indicate some ways by which it may be remedied.

PART THREE

Distribution

CHAPTER V

The Act of Publication

Publication and Creation

T HE HISTORY of the publication of the book and the history of the book are not to be confused. Printed or not, the book is only the most recent and most widespread of ways to reproduce a literary work for dissemination; but it is not the only way. The production of a play, for example, demonstrates that the act of publication can be implemented in a society that cannot read.[1] Today the movies, radio and television render audio-visual publications more effective than printed publications.

The semantic accordance of the word *publish* with its Latin ancestor *publicare* gives us the idea of a "release" at the disposal of an anonymous public. *Publicare simulacrum* implies the raising of a statue on a public square, the publishing of matrimonial bans, the making known to all persons, anonymous or not, a project which is private by its very nature. The oldest use of this word cited by Littré dates from the thirteenth century and, applied to furniture, signifies "selling at a public auction."

Let us retain this idea of the public auction of a work, this deliberate and almost brutal exposure of the secret of creation to the anonymous light of the public square. There is implied a kind of willful violence, an accepted profanation, all the more shocking to common sensitivity in that it brings

---

1. The theatre poses special problems with which we cannot deal in this short study. We must hope to see a sociology of the theatre. We have, however, taken examples from the theatre when problems common to all forms of literature were analyzed.

financial considerations into play. To publish a work drawn from oneself for commercial reasons is a bit like prostituting oneself. *Publicare corpus*, says Plato.

But further, to publish a work is to complete it by abandoning it to others. In order to exist as an autonomous and free creation, a work must be detached from its creator and follow alone its destiny among men. Such is the symbolism of the grand opening or of the *vernissage* of paintings in an art exhibit; by varnishing his work, the painter forbids himself further retouching. He abdicates his position as guardian of his work and declares it born in hanging it from the moulding for sale.

For it is indeed a birth. ˜ This act of violent creation is a delivery: a tearing asunder, at once a painful separation and the start of a new being, autonomous and free. Without undue exaggeration, we may compare the publisher's role to that of the obstetrician: he is not the source of life, nor does he carry it within himself, nor does he contribute of his flesh to its being, but without him the work, conceived and brought to the threshold of creation, could not come to exist.

This is nothing other than the essential aspect of the publisher's function. There are many others, and to complete the metaphor, our obstetrician must be a prenatal counselor, a judge of life or death for new-born babies (even an abortionist), a hygienist, a pedagogue, a tailor, a guide and . . . a dealer in slavery.

Historical Development

The publisher is a recent phenomenon in the history of literary institutions, although for a long time means of copying the written word and distributing the work have existed. Often, an author did the copying and distributing himself. Reading in public was one of the favorite modes of *publication* in Antiquity; even after the invention of the printing press, it was and still is one of the most convenient ways of trying out a work on a limited public. The most picturesque instance of distribution by an author is perhaps that of the *Yomiuri*, the father of Japanese newspapers: after having written them, the author ran them off and then sold them himself in the streets, shouting aloud main passages.

However, as far back as earliest Antiquity, there were distribution specialists. At first, these were ambulatory storytellers who recounted traditional works and who still do in countries where hawking is common. Sometimes they read their own works. Here is an incontestable form of "publication," although a limited one.[2]

Nothing of consequence existed before the advent of the book; that is to say, the book in its earliest manuscript form. In Athens as early as the Fifth Century B.C. and in Rome during the classical era, scribes' workshops (*scriptoria*) could be found where entrepreneurs had manuscripts copied. The copies were then put on sale in real bookshops. There was thus already a book industry and a book market. The largest circulation mentioned (references to this are rare) was never greater than a few hundred copies, but the idea of publishing was taking on form and substance. It is interesting to note that the Romans described publishing by the root of the verb *edere*, which means "to put into the world," "to give birth to." This sense of the word remained the same for Virgil and Ovid, but half a century later, Pliny cast a modern publisher's judgment when he spoke of *Libelli editione digni*.

As frequently happens, the idea preceded the technical means. The means in question were to lie undiscovered for fourteen centuries. With the printing press, the accent falls on publication— that is, on the availability of books to an anonymous public, rather than on the book itself. In this sense, it can be said that the publication of the Bible was one of the determining factors of the Reformation. Let us add that technical publishing was reinforced by linguistic publication, that is, the use of the vernacular.

The first printers were already publisher-obstetricians. Their choices were of a creative nature. Thus it was to Caxton that already antiquated writers such as Chaucer, Gower, Lydgate, Malory, etc., owe their resurrection to literary life, for had they been read only in manuscript form there would have been scant assurance of their being remembered by posterity.

The first printers were also businessmen, as their many "utilitarian" but marketable books prove. Nevertheless, romances of chivalry, which were certain to sell to the aristocracy, were among the favorites to come from Caxton's press.

---

2. The limitation in question is due to the form of the distributed work, not to the area of distribution, which may be considerable and may be more extensive than that of a printed book, For while a book has need of a bookstore or library, a story-teller needs only a village square.

His successor, Wynkyn de Worde, established a store for retail sales on Fleet Street, and this was one of the first bookstores in the modern sense of the word in England.

At the end of the fifteenth century there already existed large commercial enterprises like one owned by Anton Koburger, a printer from Nuremberg. He owned sixteen bookstores and had agents in the principal cities of Christendom. Aldo Manuzio of Venice is another example of a man who flourished in the book trade. In the sixteenth century, there was the dynasty of the Estiennes in France and, in Holland, the Plantins and the Elzevirs. We know the part played by the Netherlands until the eighteenth century as a center for the book market.[3] In most countries, printing corporations or guilds were formed and their activities were regulated strictly for reasons practical rather than economic.

The powerful printers, however, absorbed by the growing complexity of their industry, were quickly forced to abandon retail sales to specialists, to delegate to the latter the operation of all or part of their commercial functions. By the second half of the sixteenth century the word *libraire* in France was no longer used to designate the functions of a copier, nor to refer to librarians (the English word, library, however, retains the original meaning). Around that time, the bookseller made his entry into English commercial life as the *Buchhandler* did in Germany.

The frontier was nevertheless not carefully delineated between the two professions, and licenses for Letters Patent in 1618 in France place printers and booksellers in a single group. Up to the end of the eighteenth century, it is difficult to assign either moral or financial responsibility to either or to decide which one would assume the risk of investing and answer for various claims that might be brought against a work. Traditionally, this thankless job fell on the shoulders of the printer, but as time went by the bookseller had to accept his share of it. In the beginning of the nineteenth century, Napoleonic legislation put an end to the debate by designating, to the profit of a third middleman, a responsible publisher for every publication— the equivalent of the mythical manager of French newspapers.

But at this date, the publisher had already been functioning for half a century: he was the manager who, relegating to the printer the technical side of the operation and

---

3. "Dutch bookstores make millions every year because the French were witty." Voltaire, *Mélanges littéraires*.

to the bookseller the commercial side of it, coordinated manufacturing with sales specifications, dealt with the author and various sub-contractors and, generally, set in order the isolated acts of publication. This action implemented the manager's general business policy. In other words, capitalistic exploitation was substituted for the exploitation of the artisan.

The substitution may be explained by the economic, political and cultural upsurge of the middle class. As we have already seen, literature ceased to be the privilege of men of letters at that time. The newly arrived middle class was demanding a literature to suit its own standards. The reading public became larger while a revolution took place in taste. Henceforth, realistic and sentimental novels, pre-romantic and romantic poems became works in large editions with tremendous circulation, the financing of which required the introduction of the powerful economic system that was succeeding so well in other areas of industrial and commercial activity.

The publication in 1740 of Richardson's *Pamela*, the prototype of the English novel, was an excellent example of capitalistic enterprise applied to the publishing industry. Richardson was President of the Corporation of Stationers, a sort of official printer for the British Government. Two of his colleagues in London, Rivington and Osborn, associated with him to publish a collection, destined for middle-class ladies, of model letters of the "perfect secretary" type. Richardson, gifted as a writer, was to furnish the text himself. This was a perfect example of utilitarian publication. From that text, by a series of transformations, Richardson's genius created *Pamela*, an epistolary novel, spawned by the non-literary initiative of a group of book manufacturers and businessmen.

Among present publishing houses, a number have begun in such a way. For example, the house of John Murray accompanied the rise of British romanticism. Other publishing houses, such as Plon in France, developed from the printing press; but some, like Hachette, began as bookstores and grew into publishing houses. There still exist printer-publishers and bookseller-publishers.

During the first half of the twentieth century, the function of the publisher underwent a last transformation, particularly in France, which corresponds to the decline of capitalism and to the rise of the masses. Many publishers, dismayed by the costs of promotion and distribution, turned over this part of their business to specialized enterprises such as Hachette or Chaix. It is still difficult to evaluate the effect of this practice on the evolution of the publisher's function.

The Publisher's Function

Reduced to their material operations, the publisher's functions can be summed up in three verbs: choose, manufacture and distribute. These three operations are linked together, each depending on the others while they condition one another; they form a cycle which constitutes the act of publication.

To each of these operations correspond respectively the three essential services of a publishing firm: those of the literary committee, the manufacturing office and the commercial department. The publisher coordinates their actions, gives them meaning and assumes responsibility for them. Even when the publisher remains anonymous and the policy of a house is fixed by an administrative council, there must be an individual— a director, a counselor or an administrator — to give the publishing act the personal and united character which is indispensable to it.

A publisher remains a publisher even should he delegate to specialists his diverse technical functions, such as the selection, manufacture and distribution of books. It is essential, however, that he be responsible for the moral and commercial aspects of the whole undertaking.

The unique problem of publishing is that of bringing an individual fact to the community, and each of the technical functions enumerated above corresponds to a relationship between the individual and the community.

Selection presupposes that the publisher— or his delegate— imagines a possible public and chooses from the mass of writing which is submitted to him the works best suited for that public. This sort of conjecture has a twofold and contradictory nature: on the one hand, it involves a judgment of fact as to what exactly the possible public desires, what it will buy; and on the other hand, a value judgment as to what *should be* the public's taste. It must take into account the esthetic and moral systems of the human group in which the operation is performed. Two questions arise which are asked about all books, and to which the answers can be only a hypothetical compromise: Is the book saleable? Is it good?

Caught between the authors' desires and the public's demands, whatever he imagines them to be, the modern publisher does not limit himself to the passive role of conciliator. He attempts to influence his authors in the interest of the public and the public in the interest of the author; in a word, he tries to induce a compatible writer-public relationship.

The ideal thing for a publisher is to find a writer who "follows-up." In fact, once the hazards and costs of launching him are undertaken and the effectiveness of the writer is established, he can be expected, without too much risk, to produce works similar to a first well-tried specimen. Having signed a long-term contract, the author then takes his place in the publisher's "stable." It is this stable which, assuming a collective policy, gives its tone and style to the publishing house. It is, in general, dominated by one person, the publisher himself (Julliard), or one of his advisors (Jean Paulhan at Gallimard). With a team of readers (who are often writers for the house), the stable determines the selection and even influences the output of new writers who wish to become part of it.

The publisher further influences the public by instigating new patterns and habits. These habits may take the form of fashions, fads, even of a temporary infatuation with an author's personality, or they may have deeper origins and indicate predilections for certain thoughts, styles or types of literature. One of the oldest and most typical of such literary habits, consciously kept up if not entirely initiated by a publisher, was "Byronism."[4]

A particularly profitable formula is that of the specialized collection which boasts a unity of direction, presentation and interest. On the one hand, it permits the channeling of authors towards types of writing in which they have already proved themselves; on the other hand, it satisfies a well-

---

4. "Byronism" is a fashion that was launched by the publication of the first two cantos of *Childe Harold;* its characteristics had been carefully adapted to the needs of the romantic public by the wishes of the publisher, John Murray. Afterwards it was impossible for Byron to disengage himself from this legend. Murray urged him to write the same kind of literature and always arranged not to publish any of Byron's works that might shock the reading habits of his "Haroldian" public.

defined, omnipresent, precise demand. Examples of this are the *Série Blême* published by Gallimard and Hachette's *Vies Quotidiennes*.

One can go even further and define one's public in the interest of controlling it to a greater degree and of establishing quasi-personal links between it and one's stable of authors. This is done usually for genres with particularly well-marked traits such as the detective novel, the science fiction novel, the suspense novel, etc., by means of specialized magazines, book clubs, or special interest bulletins. As a result, a doctrine and an esthetic of any given genre are created, and the author-public community then possesses the characteristic of every nascent collective consciousness: orthodoxy.[5]

It must be remembered, therefore, that each selection presupposes a theoretical public in the name of which and for whose benefit it is made, and it also presupposes a sampling of writers which is supposed to reflect the needs of that public. The whole literary game played by the publisher takes place in the closed circle of these two groups which are, as we have seen, defined in advance.

Manufacturing is part of the game as well. From the beginning of the study, preliminary to actual manufacturing, the public must be kept constantly in mind. Depending on whether the house is thinking in terms of a handsome volume destined for a few hundred bibliophiles or a popular, cheap book, everything changes: the paper, the format, the typography (the choice of characters, the thickness of pages, etc.), the illustrations, the binding, and especially, the number of copies to be printed. From this moment on, the publisher must calculate the profit he hopes to make from his work. In fact, he must have calculated it back at the selection stage. Chosen because of special qualities and for a special public, the book must have well-defined and appropriate material characteristics.

The size of the edition is obviously the most important of these characteristics. If the number of copies printed is insufficient, the manufacturing costs (reading and preparation of the manuscript, composition, proof-reading, paging, type-setting) will be spread over an inadequate number of copies. These costs are by far the heaviest in each venture and determine the sales price, which, if too high, may put

---

5. Two typical examples are to be found in France, *Fiction* and *Mystère Magazine*, both published by the same company. In England, the venerable Hakluyt Society brings together those interested in adventure stories and encourages them to write.

the work out of the reach of its eventual public. If too many copies are printed, the supply will be immediately swollen and a deficit caused by lack of sales will be inevitable, for the book industry is one of the rare businesses in which the unsold manufactured product has less value than the raw material.[6]

As for the other characteristics of the work, not only must the size of the theoretical public be taken into account, but also its nature, its functional needs and, in particular, its behavior patterns. The use of the illustrated cover recently came to France from America. In the choice of a cover the publisher must be aware of the diverse motivations which induce an eventual client to purchase a book. In fact, if the drawing is well-chosen, it will constitute a true lesson in literary criticism and translate graphically the publisher's esthetic and psychological analysis which guided his selection.[7]

Here we find the advantages of the "collection" series whose presentation and optimum size of edition have been studied in advance once and for all.

For the publisher, manufacturing continues the selective process, as we can see. The judgment he has imposed on the book now takes form. He now transposes technically, through material decisions, that balance which from the beginning he has attempted to establish between the writers he proposes and the public which he supposes or creates.

The distribution of the work remains, that is, the sale itself, although gratuitous distribution of books does exist. Indeed, the sale of the book is almost indispensable to the completion of the literary fact. Byron remarked one day that to force a perfect stranger to take money out of his pocket (a gesture neither involuntary nor indifferent) to buy a book is the veritable consecration of the writer and a sign of his power.

In capitalistic countries, distribution is the most delicate part of the publishing act, everything converging towards it

---

6. A work of literature is not profitable unless it sells between 5,000 and 6,000 copies; at least 2,000 copies must be sold for the publishing house to break even.

7. The choice of title is essential to the sale of a book. As for the cover, it is much used for publicity purposes in France. It should principally reflect the title or directly reach one of the reader's motivations for reading. More intellectual but equally effective is the process which consists in analyzing the book on the dustjacket or on the back of the book. This is particularly aimed at browsers.

like a play moving towards its dénouement. It determines success or failure. In a book's budget, distribution costs represent more than half of the sales price.[8]

The publisher finds himself confronted by a difficult problem: that of finding and truly reaching the theoretical public which he has supposed or cultivated from the beginning. For this purpose, he employs a certain number of advertising techniques.

The first and the most simple is the inclusion of the book in a bibliographical list, the kind that exists in most countries (for example the *Bibliographie de France,* a monthly publication of the *Cercle de la Librairie*). There booksellers and librarians will learn of the book's publication; personal contact with traveling salesmen, equipped with specimen copies, doubles the advertising value of this anonymous publicity. Commercial advertising of a normal kind (in newspapers, even posters or shopwindow displays) is directed at the public. This type of publicity is less common in France or England than in the United States. In the latter country, for example, the sales campaign is handled, *mutatis mutandis,* much the same way as that of any other commercial product.[9]

The inconvenience of ordinary advertising techniques is that they address the public at large and not the particular public at which the publisher aims. Of one thousand persons reached by publicity, there are perhaps about ten or twenty who may be expected to take an interest in the book, while the whole thousand may be interested in a brand of soap, or of liquor, or in a household article. For advertising to be profitable, it must be directed at those ten or twenty persons who might be influenced, however uncertainly, by its sales pitch. Unfortunately, one can never be sure of the number of persons influenced, whether two or twenty, and furthermore their identity always varies with the kind of book offered. Thus we return to the *limited* and *personal* nature of the publishing act. And for this reason advertising which is directed at a certain group— especially in signed newspaper reviews— is preferable to mass advertising. Most effective may be the article by a literary editor or the column of a critic whose clientele of readers usually subscribes to his tastes. Publishers pay particular attention to press services; each volume, signed by the author, is accompanied by a

8. In the *Monographie de l'édition* will be found complicated tables used to determine the retail sales price of a book. Briefly, the publishing cost after printing must be multiplied by a coefficient which varies from three to five.

9. The *Encyclopedia Britannica* indicates that publicity represents ten per cent of the production cost in an American publishing house. Percentages are six per cent in England and three per cent in Germany.

review of the "please insert" type, and this review is a model feature article (laudatory, of course). Many minor periodicals are content to use it as is and to add a signature to it. Infinitely more interesting is the review of a publishing house critic in a newspaper having a clientele corresponding approximately to the publisher's theoretical public. All means of pressure are exerted to obtain such a review, for the most fecund of critics can scarcely produce more than two hundred reviews a year. It matters little that the review is unfavorable; as long as the book is talked about, even a bad review may be as profitable as a good one. Thus a literary "catastrophe" may be worth a fortune.

Television, with its direct and personal appeal, has introduced extraordinarily efficacious criticism, and here the author himself confronts his public face to face. It has been ascertained that in the hours that follow the televised interview of an author, the sale of his book increases in what may reach considerable proportions.

To these diverse advertising techniques should be added those which consist of promoting a selection— for example, the choice of the best book of the month or the literary prize. One or two votes for a well-known prize is an advantage not neglected on the book's dustjacket.

Another procedure is more difficult to manage because of its ambivalent implications: the publication of a book in a newspaper or magazine either *in extenso*, in the form of excerpts, or in the form of a résumé. The very delicate problem consists of piquing the reader's interest without injuring the appeal of the work.[10]

The goal of all these techniques is to flush out the hypothetical, hidden public which is scattered among the population at large. Naturally, it would be ideal to discover and contain that public and to keep it contained as a group once and for all. This is the rationale of book clubs, whose ultimate aim is to substitute the "ready-made" for the "'custommade." Once found, catalogued, sometimes even bound by contract, the reader can no longer escape.

The same is true in dictatorships and, especially, in socialistic countries. In the U.S.S.R., for example, the unsold book is relatively rare, for as competition does not exist a publisher has the means of adapting circulation to demand and demand to circulation.

In capitalistic countries, the publisher's situation is much more precarious. From the moment the book is put on sale,

---

10. The *Notebooks of Major Thompson* was one example of successful pre-publication, helped by its publication at *irregular intervals* in *Le Figaro*.

its fate is no longer in the publisher's hands. The sale of a book is regulated by special mechanisms in the book industry: we shall discuss this point further on. The book behaves somewhat like those first teleguided rockets, most of which fell before taking their planned trajectory, while others went out of control completely and flew off erratically and unpredictably. In the same way, the majority of books published in France (60 to 70 per cent), fall out of the market before reaching a profitable volume of sales— and the publisher can do nothing about it. From time to time, a work crosses beyond the most optimistic, predictable boundaries and becomes a best seller. Sales curves vary in apparently undecipherable rhythms as soon as they break through a critical boundary (in general, in France, the "100,000 wall"). The publisher then can do nothing but blindly follow the first edition with others.

The reason for the publisher's lack of control is clear enough: it occurs when the work passes the limits of the hypothetical public for which it was conceived. It evolves then in unprospected and unsurveyed regions. The impossibility of foreseeing reactions at this moment illustrates the weakness of the system.

The act of publication is creative only in appearance. In reality, it takes place in a closed circuit within one social group. A work not adapted to this group fails; it is unlikely that it will find a more sympathetic public elsewhere— indeed, the very nature of the publisher's initial choice makes this inconceivable. We shall see that this "second" public sometimes appears without forewarning due to a "creative betrayal," but it does not depend on the publisher.

Nor does the phenomenon of success depend on him either. It is as rare as it is unpredictable. Let us remember that of 100,000 works in France between 1945 and 1955, scarcely one out of a thousand broke through the "100,000 wall." It can be seen that the publisher has no more positive influence on the destiny of his new-born work than the obstetrician with whom we have compared him. Nevertheless, his negative influence is considerable, for the beings he brings into the world enjoy only an artificial liberty strictly limited to the social circuit for which they have been delivered.

CHAPTER VI

The Circuits of Distribution

The Limits of the Circuit

THERE IS no direct relationship between the value of a book and the size of its public, but there is a strong one between the existence of a book and the existence of a public. Similarly, the value of the currency issued by a country is not measured by the size of its population, yet a currency has no meaning without reference to a specific country in which it is used.

What are the currency frontiers of a book? The first two which spring to mind are those of language and illiteracy. To understand the language of a book and to be capable of reading it are two conditions indispensable to its use.

In R. E. Barker's *Books For All*, there is an outline of a study of this problem, which might merit further research.

The large linguistic blocks of the *reading* public are the English (208 million, around 1950), the Russian (136 million), the Chinese (132 million), the Japanese (77 million), the German (74 million), the Spanish (62 million) and the French (52 million). Within each of these blocks exists an autonomous literary flow more or less split up by political institutions and national boundaries, but this flow is far from having everywhere the same intensity.

Translations allow for the establishment of a certain mechanical equilibrium among linguistic blocks. The systematic and regular inventory of the *Index Translationum*, published by UNESCO since 1950, will doubtlessly shed light on the governing laws which regulate trends in translation. It would appear here and now that there are three trends:

1. Ideological trends within one socio-political community. In this category fall the trends emanating from the Russian block directed towards the various linguistic units

within the USSR, or towards the minor linguistic blocks in the countries belonging to the Soviet sphere of influence, or towards the Communist minorities in the other blocks.

2. The *pooling* trends between the large-producing and large-consuming blocks. For example, the French, English and German blocks share from ten to twenty per cent of their literary production.

3. The balancing trends between high-pressure and low-pressure literary zones. The high-pressure zones are not only the large-producing blocks mentioned above, but also and especially, the little linguistic groups with an advanced culture whose overabundant literary population easily saturates the reading population and looks for an outlet through translations. Examples are the Netherlands, or the Scandinavian countries, which in 1952 produced respectively 590 and 442 indigenous titles per million inhabitants, while France produced 212 and Spain 100. As for the low-pressure zones, they are located mainly in young countries with high birth rates where the rapid cultural evolution of the population creates a need for reading which local production still cannot satisfy: i.e., in Japan and Latin America.

National boundaries (which do not always coincide with cultural or linguistic boundaries) offer additional frontiers to contain the distribution of books. Even in countries such as France which export heavily, whether translations or original works, the great majority of production is reserved for the internal market. Protective customs regulations (notably between countries competing in one linguistic block, such as the United Kingdom and the United States) and monetary restrictions emphasize the "Balkanization" of literature. But even the more liberal laws sought by UNESCO would not solve the problem. For law considers the book only as a material object and weighs nothing but its worth as a manufactured artifact. In reality, account should be taken of the real worth of cultural exchange depending on the milieu or the group. According to the economic and social structure of any two countries, and to the place the cultural function occupies in their national hierarchies of values, a given book does not have the same significance, the same definition, from one country to the other.[1]

The mechanism of literary distribution must then be studied in relation to spheres both more general and more simple than nations or linguistic blocks, which are already complex structures. Actually, every social group possesses its own cultural needs, and consequently its own literature.

---

1. In achieving an *Atlas of Reading in Bordeaux* at the *Centre de Sociologie de Faits littéraires,* the topographical existence of both circuits has been demonstrated.

A group may be determined by sex, age, class; then we might speak of women's literature, children's literature, and proletariat literature. Each of these literatures has its own particular system of distribution, but although women's magazines, children's bookstores and libraries for workers do exist, these literatures are far from having their own institutions. There are overlapping situations and double uses, even mutations, which cause transfers of certain works from one classification to another.

The social group which has the clearest literary identity is the cultured group. As a matter of fact, we have seen that the category of "cultivated" readers is at the basis of the very idea of literature. The cultured class, which originally constituted a closed caste, is neither identified today with a caste, nor a social stratum, nor even a socio-professional group. Cultured people may be defined as persons having received an intellectual training and an esthetic education advanced enough to enable them to exercise literary and personal judgments, having sufficient time to read, and having enough money to buy books with regularity. Let us note that this is a potential definition, not a real one: many cultured individuals have no literary opinions, never read and never buy books— but they *could*.

This cultured group used to correspond to the aristocracy. Later it was identified with the cultivated middle-class whose cultural bulwark was classical secondary education. The group has now been increased by intellectuals (notably members of the teaching profession who constitute its majority), workers in the arts and— albeit in very small part — manual laborers educated at elementary or vocational levels. This group corresponds to what we have called the "literary milieu," from which most writers are recruited. From that milieu, as well, are recruited all the participants in the literary fact ranging from the writer to the literary historian of the university, from the editor to the literary critic. The people who "make" literature are all cultured people. The cultured literary fact revolves in a closed circuit within this group, as we have seen in studying the mechanism of the act of publication.

In opposition to the "cultured circuit," we shall give the name of popular circuit (for want of a better word) to those networks of distribution meant for readers (in the socio-professional categories) whose upbringing endows them with an intuitive literary taste, but not with an explicit or reasoned power of judgment. The conditions of their work and existence make reading an unwonted or uncomfortable activity, and their lack of resources prohibits the purchase of many books. These readers sometimes belong to the lower middle class, but the majority are employees, manual laborers and farmers. Their literary needs are of the same importance, type and quality as those of cultured readers, but these needs are always satisfied by outsiders. They themselves have no way of making known their reactions to those writers or publishers responsible for literary output. While an exchange of ideas occurs in the cultured bookstore, the basic establishment in popular circuits is a book outlet or a simple sales location. There, readers do not participate in the literary game.

The Cultured Circuit

Let us take the example of a fairly large bookstore, one of thousands which exist everywhere in the world. Its present stock includes from 5,000 to 6,000 titles, usually with one or a maximum of two copies of each. Of the stock on hand, 400 are in the show window and 1,200 are on the shelves inside the store.

French production of books is from 10,000 to 12,000 titles per annum. Even if business is good and the stock is rapidly replenished, one can hope to find only a fraction of these titles in that bookstore. A fraction of that fraction is offered on racks within the store to the client interested enough to go inside, that is, one already integrated into the commercial bookstore circuit. It is a minute fraction of this fraction which, during a rather short period of time, is on display for the public-at-large.

This situation implies that the bookseller, like the publisher, selects from the mass of writings available to him only titles which he feels his limited public may consume. The bookseller's selection will differ from the publisher's in that the latter's public is hypothetical, while the bookseller's public is real and manifests itself directly as customers. Another difference is that the manuscript rejected by the publisher does not attain literary existence, while the book not put on sale by this or that bookseller already exists and continues to exist. In other words, the publisher's choice creates literature, while that of the bookseller determines degrees of its saleability.

There are bookstores whose stock and especially whose system of supply are adapted to any kind of demand,[2] but they are very few indeed. One statistic dating from 1945,

---

2. The bookseller's problem, when he orders from a publisher, is to avoid the transportation costs which can absorb the greater part of his profit. So large bookstores use transport agents who collect many books at a time. Obviously, the problem does not occur for those bookstores situated near publishers' warehouses or for those which belong to publishing houses themselves. In certain countries (the Netherlands, Denmark, Norway and Switzerland), there are distribution centers of a cooperative type.

cited by the *Monographie de l'édition*, counts 203 "general assortment" bookstores in France. There has been no substantial variation of this number by 1957. There are large enterprises which, by definition, keep an abundant, varied stock on hand and can, in certain exceptional cases, transcend 100,000 volumes.

In France, the bookstore, like publishing houses, is a relatively small enterprise. In strongly capitalistic countries, especially England, Germany, and the United States, there exist huge concentrations of books such as that of Basil Blackwell at Oxford. These concentrations presuppose enormous capital assets. For their part, socialistic countries, where the bookstore is exempt from commercial hazards, have created in their large cities book warehouses where the assortment (within the rather narrow limits of editions still in stock) is as complete as possible.[3]

Such enterprises are often difficult to manage. The always menacing presence of unsold books can completely depreciate the value of the business in a few months of careless selling policies. For this reason, whatever their size, large bookstores have been obliged to keep personal contact with their customers by sending periodic catalogues, by man-to-man communication, by specialization in certain departments or branch offices, and also by granting permission to prospective customers to browse among the shelves.[4] Therefore, the favored business zones in which to begin a general bookstore are urban areas where the proximity of a university sustains an intense intellectual life. In France, for example, these would be, in order of their importance, the sixth, eighth, seventh, and fifth *arrondissements* of Paris; then Lille, Lyons, Bordeaux, Marseilles, Strasbourg, Toulouse, etc.

The medium-sized bookstore has the job of distributing "literary" books in its territory. There are about 3,500 medium-sized bookstores in France, or one for every 12,000 inhabitants. This number is certainly one of the highest in the world.[5] In some countries the number of sales points may

---

3. In the Soviet Union publishing houses belong to the State or to unions, the largest being the Union of Writers. Distribution is centralized by the Ministry of Culture, which services the 25,000 bookstores in the Union and libraries, as well as providing sales by correspondence.

4. Gilbert's Bookstore in France is an excellent example of these diverse commercial procedures.

5. In 1945 the *Monographie de l'édition* counted 203 bookstores with a general selection, 2,611 medium-sized bookstores, 4,976 small bookstores, and estimated that there were 17,000 sales points. *Books For All* gives 3,535 "real" bookstores for 1952, with an average staff of twelve persons, and 12,780 bookstores including newspaper stands. For the same year, *L'Annuaire statistique de la France* counted 7,348 establishments involved in the book trade (decimal classification 764) of which 5,690 had less than six employees. These figures demonstrate the extreme difficulty of making evaluations without even one valid criterion.

indeed be greater, but we are dealing here with bookstores having an original and autonomous commercial policy.

This autonomy and liberty assume the presence of stocks large enough to permit commercial handling, but limited enough so that unnecessary quantities of capital are not tied up. The bookstore suits its stock, as we have seen, to the needs of its customers. By examining a shop window, one can predict the proximity of a university, a cathedral, a *lycée*, a factory, or a theater, and even have a rough idea of social and professional characteristics of the surrounding population.

Specialization is one of the procedures by which a medium-sized bookstore directs and limits its activities. A typical and frequent instance is that of the classical bookstore operating near an academic establishment. Most often, the bookstore expands its business by including sales of stationery and school supplies. In many cases, the list of books used in classes is established by the school together with the bookseller, who then knows well in advance the nature and volume of orders to make. The system offers the school the advantage of seeing its demands satisfied immediately. This kind of symbiosis exists each time a bookstore finds itself in contact with a social organism having regular and valuable functional reading needs. Besides classical bookstores, there are technical, religious, medical bookstores, etc., where distribution occurs in a closed cycle within a narrow community.

Another kind of specialization is that of the art bookstore which very often also sells used books. The proportion in used books can be evaluated at seven to eight per cent, but for the moment, the used book business has eluded all statistics; it is still fertile ground for research. Limited to a small number of booklovers, it has but a weak influence on true literary consumption, except in a certain number of individual cases which we shall discuss later.

Medium-sized bookstores which sell new literary books are more evenly distributed than general-assortment establishments. Every small town of any size has its own medium-sized bookstore. In the Department of Gironde, for example, the proportion is 1 for 10,000 inhabitants in and around Bordeaux and 1 for 11,000 in the department.

But actually the medium-sized bookstore, as soon as it leaves the domain of functional reading, directs itself only toward certain well-defined social levels. It is notably not aimed at the working class, nor at the peasant class. As Bénigno Cacérès remarks: "Bookstores which sell quality novels . . . are not located on the working man's path except on rare occasions."[6] In his daily rounds, the worker runs across the newspaper stand, the tobacco store, the five and dime, the street pedlar's display, and it is from these sources that he occasionally draws reading materials.

The comparison of the show-window of a medium-sized neighborhood bookstore with that of a "book-outlet" (newspaper vendor or tobacco store) located in the same section of the city is revealing. Both displays coincide in certain types of books, the kinds of works whose social gamut is extensive, such as detective novels, best-sellers which have broken the "100,000 wall," the great literary classics in cheap editions, etc., but the bulk of their stock differs radically. Nobody would think of asking for Péguy at the tobacco store, or at the bookstore for the latest "heart-throb" novel that sells for five cents. What is more serious is that the worker and the intellectual, both buying *Major Thompson*, will not go to the same establishment.

We will return to "book-outlets." For the moment, let us just remember that the immense majority of medium-sized bookstores corresponds to what we have called the circuit of cultured literature— the kind of literature that aspires eventually to be found in literary textbooks. Their customers include particularly members of the educated middle-class and of the artistic, intellectual or liberal professions, that is, a reading population in France from one to two million people, of the total reading population of twenty-five million.

We will have a better idea of the scantiness of the cultured circuit by examining the list of French works in 1956 which sold more than 10,000 copies. This list was published by the *Nouvelles littéraires*.[7] It is not exhaustive but clearly contains almost all the essential literary reading material that fed Frenchmen of the cultured class that year. The following facts are evident:

1. The total number of copies represented on the list is 4,300,000 of the approximately 150 million copies put into circulation by the French printing press; or, roughly, 3 per cent.

2. The list comprises 166 titles from 3,000 classified as "literary," or 3.5 per cent.

3. Nineteen publishers are represented on the list from among some 750 who could be considered as active in 1956, or 2.5 per cent.

---

6. "Comment conduire le livre au lecteur?" *Informations sociales* (January 1957), p. 107. Cacérès is a specialist in "popular" education.

7. *Les nouvelles littéraires*, January 31, 1957.

Of course, we are taking neither functional books into account, nor minor successes and failures, nor universal literary reading matter (of the detective novel type) from which most booksellers make their living. But these indications suffice to demonstrate that what we term the literary life of a country such as France (where it is particularly energetic) is an activity in which only a small number of participants engage.

Without always being aware of it, the bookseller is one of the leaders in this activity. The commercial equilibrium of his enterprise forces him to exercise constant vigil not only on production (mainly in reading new books to which the critics have drawn his attention) but also on reactions of customers who often seek his advice. In general an influential person in his town or neighborhood, he is, for the local *intelligentsia*, a literary advisor: polls show that the bookseller's advice is one of the decisive factors in the launching of a successful book (its development being more or less out of his hands). For the publisher, in addition, he is the barometer of popular taste. In France, for example, those publishers are rare who would infringe upon the taboo cast by bookstores on short story collections— for perfectly explicable commercial reasons.

To complete the picture of the cultured circuit, a last link must be discussed— the literary critic. Authors often speak ill of him and publishers tend to fear him. He merits neither this excess of homage nor such indignity. The true role of literary criticism should be that of the public's sampler. The critic belongs to the same social milieu as the cultured reader and has the same education. He has a variety of political, religious and esthetic opinions, a diversity of temperaments which are reflections of those found in the reader, but he has the same culture and way of life. Without even considering his critical judgement, the mere fact that he writes about certain works and not of others is already a significant choice: good or bad, a book "people are talking about" is one socially adapted to a group. If the critic's most frequent error is to disdain books which later become bestsellers (rarely the contrary), it is exactly because a bestseller, as we have seen, is a book which passes beyond the limits of the group.

The so-called education of taste by the critic only makes explicit the diverse orthodoxies which govern the behavior of the cultured public. One has but to study the buyer of newspapers. There the great "creative" critics preach to converts and hardly ever reach those who might possibly need an "education," that is, a training analagous to theirs. It is obvious that the ascendency of some critics (particularly those who write in provincial papers for a public difficult to define) allows them to exercise an influence on reading choice, but polls prove again that this influence is no stronger than that of the bookseller nor, especially, that of the most frequently mentioned literary advisors: the Parisian cousin, the teacher or the priest.[8]

As far as the publisher is concerned, criticism has the objective value of a literary opinion of which it is the spokesman. The pre-criticism of reading committees is modeled quite simply on professional criticism, and each publisher wishes to have a group of readers which is a sampling of that hypothetical public whose reflection will guide his selections.

The circuit of cultured literature thus presents the appearance of a series of successive choices, each one limiting the other. The publisher's choice of his authors' works limits the choice of the bookseller, who then limits the reader's choice. The reader's choice is reflected on the one hand by the bookseller in his commercial department and expressed by criticism on the other hand, then translated and amplified by the reading committee, thus limiting in its turn future selections by the publisher and, consequently, possibilities offered to talented authors.

This negative interaction encloses its participants in an ever-shrinking circle. The concentration of talent and material means in this reduced social zone leads to regrettable waste. If it is improbable that reading committees have ever totally ignored great talents, it is certain that a number of excellent books have not benefited from the opportunity they merited, due to the lack of a sufficiently extensive distribution at the beginning. The large proportion of failures to which the biggest publishers attest (possibly from 60 to 70 per cent of published works), in a country where 80 per cent of the population is culturally undernourished, proves that distribution in a closed circuit offers only the alternative of waste or sterilization.

Popular Circuits

Commercial distribution of literary works to the masses is assured principally by book outlets. Within this term are included the little bookstores and establishments such as tobacco stores or newspaper stands for which the sale of books is a secondary occupation. Depending on whether

---

8. This information, based on polls, is subject to verification and deals only with France. It is contradicted by that of the German publisher, Eugen Diedrich, obtained by a poll conducted through the mail in 1930. Book reviews are mentioned by seventeen to eighteen per cent of the readers, friends or relatives by fourteen to seventeen per cent, booksellers by only five to seven per cent.

we add subordinate sales points such as shelves in stores like the Monoprix (a five- and ten-cent store), their number in France varies from 4,000 to 16,000 or 17,000. This category virtually fades out at the end, and it is difficult to assign a fixed minimum criterion to it. We would have to count temporary racks of second-hand booksellers, traveling salesmen, hawkers, etc. Certain indications make us believe that the total number of sales points, all types of bookstores included, would be around 100,000![9]

Such a number obviously affords maximum territorial distribution. In the United States where the number of large- and medium-sized bookstores is three or four times less than in France in proportion to their respective populations, drug stores in cities and general stores in small towns furnish an extremely dense commercial network which the publisher exploits.

In addition, the association of the book trade with other businesses (stationery, newspapers, tobacco, food, etc.) places the book in the path of everyday life. No one has to make the effort to enter a bookstore any more. That effort is still less when books are proposed at the moment the reader has leisure time to read: at the newspaper stand in the railway station, at the tobacco store on the way home from work, from the traveling salesman, or even at home from door-to-door chapmen.

The chapman is an individual fast disappearing in our countries, killed by rapid means of communication— but he still exists and plays an important part in countries where distribution of books is still inadequate to the new cultural needs of the masses (notably in Latin America). In China the Communist regime has even integrated him with its official distribution policy. In Charles Nisard's book, previously cited, *Histoire des livres populaires ou de la littérature de colportage*, precious information will be found concerning the "chapman circuit" about the middle of the nineteenth century in France, with its principal centers of production

9. We are including certain long-term sales points in this number, such as fairs, carnivals, bazaars, etc. The graph of sales points (decimal category 764) compared with that of large bookstores reveals curious differences. While the number of large bookstores is great (outside Paris) in the Nord, the Bas-Rhin, the Rhône, the Gironde and the Bouches-du-Rhône (departments with universities), the Midi (and particularly the South-East) would appear to be the richest zone in sales points. It has three especially dense concentrations in the Rhône, the Hautes-Pyrénées and Haute-Garonne, and the Bouches-du-Rhône, Var and Alpes-Maritimes. It would be interesting to compare this distribution with other economic and demographic data.

and places where specialized publishers were located: Paris, Troyes, Epinal, Nancy, Châtillon-sur-Seine, Tours, Le Mans, Lille, etc.

The essential stock of this literature consists of innumerable almanacs of which the *Almanach Vermot* or the *Almanach Hachette*, in spite of several revisions, still retain their principal traits in less naïve form. Next to the almanacs in the hawker's basket were books on magic or astrology "for ladies," collections of jokes or funny sayings, works of religious, moral, sentimental and pratical counsel, as well as a few traditional cooking and medicinal recipes. Finally, there were adventures or travel stories, sentimental novels, literary classics tested by many generations and usually abridged or adapted, and, ubiquitously, illustrations which relieved the reader's attention. It is easy to see from this description that the chapman's inheritance in the middle of the twentieth century has been accepted by the women's magazine—from the horoscope to the advice to the lovelorn, along with the sentimental novel and the pervasive illustrations.

Throughout popular distribution circuits, books are associated with the daily and weekly press, which constitutes, as we have seen, the essence of reading in most countries. The press has taken the place of old oral distribution methods (these have partially come back through the audio-visual techniques of television, the movies and radio, with which the popular book has equally tight links). Thus it is normal that the distribution method of the popular book is rather the "press delivery-service" type than the bookstore type. All initiative is firmly in the hands of the wholesale distributor. The retail dealer now serves only as an agent.

We have seen that many publishers delegate a part of their commercial function to specialized enterprises, of which the best known and the largest in France is the *Messageries Hachette*. These enterprises employ a system for the press as well as for the book which places a certain number of copies automatically with subscribing retail dealers. Naturally, the service picks up unsold books as well.

This system is used (but not exclusively) by publishers and certain bookstores of the cultured circuit. It is a kind of blind net-casting. When the book appears, the distributor places some of the edition (3,000 to 5,000 copies in France) at predetermined sales points. This explains why the selection of books at the railway station newsstand may be as rich in new titles as that of a large central bookstore. But the great part of these new books will take the road back to the warehouse, sooner or later, more or less shop-soiled.

Dependable sale articles such as detective novels or sentimental novels, of which we shall have more to say later on, are incorporated into a collection or series which appear at regular intervals. Here the distribution takes on the appearance of a "subscription-sale." Each dealer knows approximately the number of copies he will sell and stocks up accordingly.

The cascade of selections which characterizes the cultured circuit has no room within this system. There is no possible "reply" from the public to the publisher. The necessary adaptation of the book to the reader's needs is obtained by a mechanical procedure of standardization. A certain type of book whose success is assured among the public will be reproduced tirelessly with but a few plot variations on the prototype. Charles Nisard in his work on the literature of hawking shows the medieval origins of certain sentimental stories reproduced again and again in brochures costing practically nothing. The negligible cost has increased to 25 or 50 *centimes*, the stories adapted to twentieth-century tastes, but the themes themselves are strictly the same in our sentimental novels. The secretary has replaced the shepherdess in the new idyll.[10]   Similarly, the theme of Richardson's *Pamela*, oversweetened and duplicated in the women's novel of the eighteenth century (Nisard cites Madame Cottin, but there are quite a few others), ends in the immense family of novels by Delly which, in themselves, constitute a literary genre and have been unbeatable best sellers for several generations.[11] Renewing the old tradition of the popular epic, Walter Scott, a needy publisher, perfected the prototype of the historical novel, which rapidly outgrew the cultured circuit to become, with the novels of Alexandre Dumas and his contemporary imitators, one of the favorites of popular literature.

In this merciless mechanism the natural movement is towards degradation. Originality and progress occur only when, by chance, a work passes beyond the limits of the cultured circuit and penetrates a larger social milieu. But as soon as this happens, it is caught in the cog-wheel, reduced to its own striking traits and crudely reproduced again and again until demand is exhausted, which may take centuries.

However, the new techniques of mass distribution have modified considerably the data of the problem in the last generation. More and more often works which would have remained imprisoned in the cultured circuit now escape with the support of the press, records, movies or radio.

---

10. Charles Nisard names a certain Raban who appears to have been the principal manufacturer (we dare not say author) of this type of novel in the nineteenth century.
11. In an article cited elsewhere, Bénigno Cacérès notes among a list of sentimental novels found on racks, a *Destin d'Inès*, a novel by Paméla. Even in 1957 the name retains its fascination.

The motion picture technique is the most frequent and most spectacular of these. "Read the book of the film" has become one of the most efficient advertising slogans. It is true that people, in general, are content with the film alone or, worse, with "the story taken from the film," which is the specialty of a certain number of magazines. Only a vast investigation would enable us to specify to what degree the movies make people read or, on the contrary, stop them from reading.

But there is no doubt that records have saved lyric poetry, which is oral by nature and was fast becoming pale and sickly on the printed page. From Villon to Prévert the popular poet has come back to his true milieu by virtue of the record player and the juke-box.

The roles of the press and the radio are more obvious. If they affect the cultured public through criticism, they act on the whole public through the infinitely more efficient methods of the serialized novel, the comic strip or adaptations. Some examples lead us to believe that the publication of a literary classic in comic-strip form in a large daily paper or the broadcast of a serial immediately provokes an affluence of buyers from the popular circuit. These influences deserve to be studied with exactitude.

The effectiveness of the press, broadcasting and movies in causing a work to enter the popular circuit derives from the kind of aptitude examination for social adaptation (sometimes disastrous) which they make all works undergo, and from the fact that they bring that work literally into the reader's daily life by placing it in the popular reader's daily path. The weakness here is that all of this takes place unilaterally, without direct intervention by a public which remains passive. This literature is a "gift."

The above situation is the inverse of that of the cultured circuit. In the latter the plethora of producers in relation to an insufficiently large consumer public, the demand which is renewed incessantly within a system based on successive selections, leads to waste and sterilization. In popular circuits the lack of socially adapted producers, the placing of all initiative in the distributor's hands, the immensity and anonymity of a demand which is not expressed but which nevertheless involves consumption lead to attrition and to the mechanical degradation of literary forms as well as to the alienation of the cultural liberty of the masses.

The problem is one of balance. Consequently, the efforts of those who try either to make cultured literature healthy or to create a true popular literature tend to demolish the barriers between popular and cultured circuits. We shall rapidly examine some of the processes used to run the social blockade of literature.

The Blockade Runners

Four types of procedures may be distinguished: traditional commercial procedures, heterodox commercial procedures, loans and authoritarian control.

Spreading the production and distribution of the cultured circuit to the popular circuit without modifying commercial methods is the simplest idea. The solution then is provided by the cheap edition of the cultured book which can be put on the level of book outlets. This is not new, for the chapman's basket already contained four-penny novels bearing the signatures of Defoe, Swift, Perrault, Florian, Bernardin de St. Pierre, etc. But most of these works were classics, not new works. Now, it is essential that no chronological lag exist, that the "poor" public participate in active literary life as well as the "wealthy" public. Several attempts at this coalition took place between the two World Wars, particularly in France. It was only in 1935 (the beginning of the five-and-ten-cent store era) that the first success occurred in England with the cheap edition form (six pence) of the Penguin collection.

The Penguin collection, directed by John Lehman, comprised more than 1,000 titles twenty years after its inauguration (an amount which accounts for only a minimal percentage of the enormous British output of literary books). Its red and white cover has become famous throughout the world. At first composed of new editions of recent hard-cover books, it is now beginning to include a few original publications in its collection. To the usual Penguin (the American version has an illustrated cover) was added the green Penguin, a series of detective novels, the blue Pelican, devoted to functional readings, and the Puffin for children. It is impossible to know the exact sales figures of the Penguin collections, but in 1955 the total mentioned was around 20 million copies per year, a figure which, if exact, accounts for seven to eight per cent of British production.

During the Second World War, the necessity of distributing reading materials to troops, and then propaganda needs, incited the United States to publish series analagous to the Penguin collection: the Signet Book, the Bantam, and especially the Pocket Book, of which France's equivalent is now the *Livre de Poche*. In most countries there are series of the same kind, whose titles, like Penguin, show respect to zoology and, particularly, ornithology: for example, the "Marabout" series in Belgium, the "Alcotan" (Falcon) in Spain (Barcelona), and the "Libri del Pavone" (Peacock) in Italy (Milan).

Their common characteristic is that they are inexpensive. Each book represents only a half hour to two hours of the average salary of a worker.

The effectiveness of the cheap book is incontestable. The Penguin collection resulted in healthy and durable effects in English literature. During World War II, the Penguin New Writing series appeared, giving new talents in difficult circumstances an opportunity to be published. But within the framework of traditional commercial methods, the cheap book is profitable (thus possible) only if it is aimed at a public vast enough to warrant huge editions. In capitalistic countries, the English linguistic block is the only one which offers sufficiently large numbers.

The solution may be, then, to get rid of the traditional book business with its inevitable and costly trio: publisher, distributor, bookseller. This is what book clubs, which we have already mentioned, are doing. In general, book clubs are not intended for the popular public, but some of them do offer classics and recent books at low prices. Unfortunately the latter are generally rather delayed new editions of books (except again in the English linguistic block), for publishers are reluctant to authorize the publication of what may be dangerous competition for books already difficult to sell. The book clubs labor, however, under a serious handicap, that of the correspondence system. However ingenious the system may be to search out new members, their response to advertising demands more of an effort than that of entering a bookstore.

Logic indicates the elimination of this effort by having salesmen go from door to door. This is to return to the chapman technique which is frequently employed to sell tomes such as dictionaries and encyclopedias. This method is more rarely applied to the sales of literary works; however some examples do exist.

In the article already quoted from *Informations sociales*, Gilbert Mury mentions the experiment of the *Jeunes Auteurs Réunis* in which he is participating. This organization rather curiously returns to the Japanese tradition of the *yomiuri*, as its authors are also its publishers and distributors; if they do not themselves sell the product, they at least attempt to make surveys of the public by means of canvassers whom they pay: "The door-to-door system is practiced by young people who ring doorbells, talk to customers of cafés and restaurants and introduce themselves to the personnel of various organizations— in particular, teachers— to whom they propose a variety of works."[12] Gilbert Mury's ingenuous "in particular, teachers," makes us think that the procedure includes a scouring of the cultured circuit, but with no real way of getting out of it. It is nonetheless certain that the *Jeunes*

12. *Informations sociales* (January 1957), p. 67.

Auteurs Réunis have achieved sales figures which many licensed publishers would envy. To eliminate the bookstore is a dream which many publishers indulge.

Whatever the merits of the door-to-door system, it can not be seriously envisaged as a means of general distribution. If all novels were to be sold in such a way, each home would have to prepare itself to receive the visit of several salesmen a day, each loaded with a bulging suitcase of specimens. The welcome mat would not stay out for very long.

In addition to sales, the loan system remains to be examined. The efficiency of loans has been proved by the success of the "loan-sale" in popular circuits. This involves the "trade-in" of a used book plus a small payment in exchange for a new book. The system is used in *Boot's* drugstores in England. It is also used by the salesman of "sentimental" novels who sets up his racks at quitting time at the factory exit.

Let us note, moreover, that the purchase of a book is economically absurd if it does not presuppose the repeated use of that book. Rare are those novels which are re-read, and even more rare are those read three or four times in one's lifetime. For the average French worker to invest in a book with no return on his investment, and which he will only read once, is to pay for a minute of reading with a minute of work or more— while movies give him more lively pleasure (especially of a social kind) at the rate of one minute of entertainment for twenty seconds of work. In other countries the difference is even greater. Thus we should not be astonished that the majority of readers in popular libraries, when asked why they frequent these establishments, answer, "The cost of books."[13]

We will not emphasize the study of libraries about which numerous and reliable studies have been made. It is sufficient to point out that public libraries are particularly well developed in England, where the number of registered readers during 1955-56 exceeded 13,500,000 and the number of works lent approached 400 million volumes. The frontiers of the cultured circuit, as one can see, are easily crossed here. In France, where central lending libraries in each department feed local libraries, the results are equally impressive. In the Department of Dordogne, in 1954, for example, 8.4 per cent of the population were members of lending libraries (the ratio of loans to members being, however, much less than in England: 5 to 1, instead of 30 to 1). Six per cent of the farmers, and five per cent of the manual workers and crafts-

---

13. This information was collected by Miss Nicole Robin during a poll of readers in Bordeaux public libraries.

men make up together 42 per cent of the registered total of readers. We should add, as we shall see later, that one registered reader represents several real readers.[14]

The trouble with library loans is that the problem of stock is infinitely more serious in a library than a bookstore. Owing to the legal obligation incurred by publishers to give copies of each published work to local administrations, and to regular and costly purchases, a central library can be assured of a general assortment. Unfortunately, a central library has a strong chance of becoming what Bénigno Cacérès calls a "graveyard of books," for it is located outside popular circuits, those of daily life. The decision to enter a central library (where, in general, a book must be read on the spot) is even more difficult a step than entering a bookstore. Thus books have to be brought to the public, either commercially (private bookmobiles, lending collections of small neighborhood bookstores, lending counters in branch stores in the English style), or administratively (public lending libraries with multiple branches, libraries at the place of work, bookmobiles, parish libraries, Sunday-school libraries, union libraries, etc.). But the stock, however rapid its rotation, remains strictly limited and subject, in the first example, to the aforementioned selection of certain booksellers, or in the second example, to that of the librarian. And the latter selection may often be stricter because it is didactic.

With the best intentions in the world, the director of a department central lending library states in her annual report: "We have never yielded to the temptation of the easiest path and we have always maintained a policy that at least one-third of loans have to be documentary works. Moreover our stock includes very few detective novels and easy sentimental works. We lend them only upon specific orders from our branches and never more than three or four are given at a time. We prefer to maintain this lending standard of quality rather than yield to the temptation of increasing our loans through an easy method."[15] This attitude fails to recognize that "the easy method"— by which is meant the mechanical and the stereotyped— exists because detective novels and sentimental novels are not integrated into a real system of producer-consumer exchange, and that their prohibition cannot but accentuate the mistake which leaves them to the pitiless mechanics of popular circuit techniques.

14. One must multiply the number of books sold or loaned by the coefficient 3.5 to obtain the number of "real" readers. We know little about "hand-to-hand" lending within a family, an apartment house or a workshop. What Bénigno Cacérès calls the "hand-to-hand" lending circuit merits a serious study.
15. The annual report of the Central Lending Library of the Dordogne (1954), presented by Madame de la Motte.

The example of Georges Simenon proves, however, that the detective novel can be both popular and cultured.

We have seen here the danger which threatens all private or public literary control: didactic concern. Therefore, businessmen or cultural organizations of a secular, religious, political or official type are powerless to establish a living popular literature, to give popular circuits a part of the over-abundant life which overflows the cultured circuit. We wrote an article on this subject in *Informations sociales*: "If these attempts, as the facts have shown us, have been failures, it is because they have all made the mistake of being exterior to the popular group. They have all rested on the idea that something must be brought to the people: spiritual leaven, a message, proof, entertainment . . . Unconsciously or not, we have neglected the fact that what we call 'literature' has been the result and not the cause of the cultural awakening of a layer of the people throughout the last three centuries; that, consequently, a really popular literature will have to come from a specifically popular culture."[16]

The Soviet regime seems to have come very close to a technical solution of the problem. Writers, whom Stalin called "engineers of the soul," are in direct contact with the masses, through the intermediary of the Communist Party, through cultural organizations, or simply through their very mode of existence. In addition, the largest possible distribution is assured: the book is everywhere, on the farm and in the factory. It is the lack of paper which limits the size of editions rather than the lack of sales. Finally, the practice of club meetings, of discussions, allows a popular literary opinion to arise and this is in turn echoed to the writers without interposing the commercial obstacle of either publisher or bookseller. Unfortunately, there is an obstacle just the same, the ideological one. Here, too, we find didacticism, so great is the temptation of all cultural organizers to adapt men to institutions rather than institutions to men. We said that the Soviet regime had found the *technical* solution to the problem: it has not as yet found the *human* solution, as the crises which sometimes shake the Soviet literary world have proved.

In the last analysis the imbalance of distribution corresponds to the imbalance of production, but these are but impartial aspects of the same problem. Institutional solutions for production, such as the "Caisse des Lettres" type or for distribution, such as the "cultural organization" type are only technical palliatives. The solution, if there is one, can be found only at the level of human group attitudes towards literature: that is, at the level of consumption.

16. *Informations sociales* (January 1957), p. 11.

PART FOUR

Consumption

CHAPTER VII

The Work and the Public

The Public

EVERY WRITER, when he sets pen to paper, has present in his mind a public, even if that public is only himself. A thing is never entirely said unless it is said to someone: this, we have seen, is the meaning of the act of publication. But it may also be affirmed that a thing cannot be said *to* someone— that is, published— unless it has at first been said *for* someone. These two "someones" do not necessarily coincide; in fact, it is rare when they do. In other words, the writer's dialogue with a public is at the very source of literary creation. But between the writer and his chosen public, there may exist very great disparities.

Thus, Samuel Pepys, who wrote only for himself in his *Diary* (his short-hand and cryptographic precautions prove it) and who was consequently his own public, was introduced to an immense public after his death by publishers (in the dignified sense of the word) who issued his work. Conversely, the Chinese novelist Lou Sin, who from 1918 to 1936 published his stories in anthologies or magazines read by only a limited circle of intellectuals or militants, wrote for tens of millions of Chinese readers (who finally listened to him on the very day the triumphant Revolution gave him a publisher worthy of his intentions).

The addressed public (the interlocutor-public) may be limited to a single person, to one individual. How many works of universal stature were only personal messages in their original form? From time to time, learned criticism discovers an author's message along with its recipient and thinks that it has explained completely the author's work. Actually, what needs explaining is how the message, while changing its recipient (and often its meaning), has retained its effectiveness. The whole difference between a literary work and an ordinary document lies in that maintained effectiveness. Let us not forget that our criterion of the literary, distinguishing it from the non-literary, is its non-functional nature. Now, the author begins an imaginary or real dialogue with his public (even though that public is sometimes himself), a dialogue which is never unmotivated and by means of which he attempts to arouse feelings, convince, inform, console, liberate, even cause despair— in any case, a dialogue with an intention. A work is functional when the addressed public coincides with the public for which the work is published. A literary work, on the contrary, brings the anonymous reader as a stranger into the dialogue. The reader is not at home and knows it; he is like an invisible being who sees everything, hears everything, feels and understands everything without having real existence in the life of a dialogue which is not his. The echoed pleasure he feels as he lets himself be carried away by the emotions, the ideas and the style is a gratuitous pleasure, for it does not involve him. All esthetic pleasure and, thus, all literary intercourse would become impossible were the public to lose the security of its anonymity, the security of distance which allows it to participate without involvement (while the writer, for his part, is inexorably involved).

In this situation subsists, in effect, all the drama of cultured literature face to face with popular reality. The intrusion of the cultured public into the creative dialogue is possible only because it is already on the spot, while the popular public is on the outside and forced to accept the dialogue literally.

The publisher in the cultured circuit aims a work at the theoretical public whose role is not limited to non-active participation; rather, it awakens the work to literary significance. This public also represents a social milieu to which the writer himself belongs and which imposes on him a certain number of determinants. For the sake of clarity, we have considered the cultured public to this point as one demographic block. It is, in reality, divided and sub-divided into social, racial, religious, professional, geographic and historical groups, into schools of thought and coteries. The modern publisher tries to identify each of his stables precisely with one segment of his public. Thus the *curriculum vitae* of a reader for Julliard of Sagan is not the same as that of a reader for Fayard of Rops. Each writer bears the weight of a possible public, vast in a greater or less degree, extended more or less in time and space.

In 1751 Charles Pinot-Duclos wrote in his *Considérations sur les moeurs de ce siècle*: "I know my public. There is no person who does not have his public, that is, a part of society of which he is a member." Very fortunately, all writers do not have as clear an inkling of their public— that would paralyze them— but they are none the less its prisoners. The narrowest links which chain the writer to his possible public are the community of culture, of assumptions, and of language.

Education serves to cement the social group. We indicated above that the principal bond in the French cultured public at the end of the nineteenth century was the community of classical, secondary education. Similarly, in the sixteenth century, among a thousand others, there was a community of humanism, and in our time there is a brotherhood of Marxism. A joke by Aldous Huxley compares culture to a family whose members conjure up memories of the illustrious persons in the family album. To adapt this to France, let us conjure up the witticisms of Uncle Poquelin, the austere wisdom of Cousin Descartes, the sonorous speeches of Grandfather Hugo, the pranks of good old Papa Verlaine. To have culture is to call all the members of the family by their first names. The outsider cannot feel at ease within the circle: he is not part of the family— that is to say, he does not have its culture (which is one way of saying that he has another one). This joke gives us a fairly exact picture of reality. The great spiritual masters who dominate cultures — Aristotle, Confucius, Descartes, Karl Marx, etc.— influence less by the effect of their thought (which is not always readily accessible to the majority of family members) than by their so-called totemic value for the origins of the group: the Frenchman who calls himself Cartesian expresses an idea not very different from that of a primitive man who calls himself part of the Leopard clan.

When Ben Jonson said of Shakespeare that he knew "small Latin and less Greek" (today in France he would have called him a grade-school dropout), he wanted to indicate his exclusion from the cultural group of the "University Wits," that is, intellectuals with a humanistic culture. In fact, even while the publics of Ben Jonson and William Shakespeare overlapped, they differed deeply in their cultural "totems." Ben Jonson's public was a minority which claimed to belong to great traditions of Antiquity. That of Shakespeare was a popular majority which was content with a kind of second- or third-hand Antiquity (through Montaigne, translated by Florio, for example), yet remaining strongly attached to the Bible and to traditions of popular wisdom as well as to the great national myths.

The cultural community entails what we call community assumptions. Each group "secretes" a certain number of ideas, beliefs, value judgments or real judgments which are accepted as evident and have no need of either justification, demonstration or apology. We rediscover here concepts like those of the *Volksgeist* and of the *Zeitgeist*. Analagous to primitive taboos, these assumptions would not often withstand scrutiny, but they cannot be questioned without shaking the moral and intellectual foundations of the group. These assumptions are the bases of group orthodoxies, but also the buttress of heterodoxies and non-conformist ideas which are never anything but relative dissidences, since total dissidence would be absurd and unintelligible. Every writer therefore is the prisoner of ideology, the *Weltanschauung* of his milieu-public: he can accept it, modify it, refuse it totally or partially, but he cannot escape it. This is why a possible public not cognizant of the fundamental assumptions of a group may misconstrue the true meaning of certain works.

Let us continue with the example of Shakespeare and consider the use he makes of ghosts and witches in his plays. Twentieth-century Western intellectuals (the category to which most Shakespearean commentators belong today) do not, in general, believe in either witches or ghosts. Consequently, they have the tendency to consider them as fantastic embellishments designed to underline the intensity of the play. Now Shakespeare's contemporaries, and particularly the public for which he wrote, believed quite naturally in what we call the supernatural. The appearance of a witch was more impressive but no more extraordinary than that of a thief. We can indeed feel in Shakespeare the scepticism of an evolved mind, but for him it was absolutely impossible to express himself otherwise than with reference to the generally admitted belief. He himself did not grasp the concept of the fantastic or the miraculous in these things because that belief presupposes that what does not conform to laws of nature is unreal, but these laws were not yet formulated in Shakespeare's time. Thus we "betray" Shakespeare (and we will see that the betrayal is necessary) if we wish to extract his work from the community of assumptions in which it was born and of which it is a prisoner.[1].

The community of assumptions within a group is determined by communal means of expression, primarily by language. At the linguistic level, a writer has at his disposal only the vocabulary and syntax which his group uses to express its assumptions. At the very most, he can "give a purer meaning to the words of the tribe," but the words of the tribe remain and cannot be separated from it without becoming distorted. From this obstacle stem the insurmountable difficulties of translation,[2] historical misinterpre-

---

1. A talk by Professor Knight of the University of Bristol, given in 1953 and entitled "The Sociology of Literature," inspired the above example.
2. The study of translation is linked to sociological aspects of literary history. The problem, however, is too immense for us to deal with here.

tations from era to era and misunderstandings from group to group within one country.

It was precisely a translation of the works of Shakespeare which recently rekindled in France the eternal controversy about translating.[3] Let us simply observe that when Ben Jonson wishes to designate the eccentricity of a temperament he uses the noble word "humour," which he borrowed from the terminology of ancient medicine. Shakespeare puts the word in Corporal Nym's mouth in *Henry V* as a kind of recurring refrain with vague magical implications, of the sort which exists in all societies on the level of the vernacular. Neither of these meanings has anything in common with "humour" today. Only a laborious, historical analysis can establish a rational relationship between the three; yet their living value remains enclosed within the limits of their respective social groups.[4]

Besides language, the group imposes other restricting determinants on the writer, such as literary genres and forms. A literary genre is not invented: it is adapted to the new demands of a social group and this justifies the idea of the evolution of genres patterned after the evolution of society. When we think of a writer as the "creator" of a genre, we too often forget that he began (perhaps at school) by pouring his inspiration into traditional molds wherein already existed the substance of the genre to which he would later give shape. Moreover, the author who illustrates a genre is rarely the one who "invented" it. He uses the tool of creation which he inherited, he gives the tool meaning, his meaning, but does not invent it. In an extreme situation, the perfect harmony of the author's temperament with the technical demands of his social group saves him from modifying his tool or even from justifying it. This observation is what the example of Racine teaches us, as explained magnificently— perhaps too magnificently— by Thierry Maulnier:

> Why would Racine revolt against a world, against a civilization, against the morals to which he so easily and happily adjusted and in which he discovered, ready and waiting, the elements of his success? . . . The tragic instrument was ready. The work of fifty years had led French tragedy not to perfection but to the hope of near and necessary

---

3. We are referring to a discussion between Yves Florenne and Dean Loiseau dealing with a translation of Shakespeare published by the *Club Français du Livre*. See *Le Monde* (August 18, 28 and September 6, 20, 24 in 1955), *Etudes anglaises* (January-March, July-September 1956) and the *Bulletin* of the *Centre d'Etudes de Littérature générale de la Faculté des Lettres de Bordeaux*, No. V.

4. L. Cazamian, *The Development of English Humor* (1951).

perfection; tragedy was waiting only for its flowering. Racine did not have the job of inventing or reconstructing, or even of leaving everything to chance, but rather the unique privilege of completing and finishing.[5]

The less definable element of style must be added to the determining factors of language and genre. In spite of the famous words of Buffon, the style is not only the man, it is also the society. Style is, in sum, the community of assumptions transposed into forms, themes and images. Style, too, has orthodoxies— academicisms— and creative dissidences which take their strength from it. Experiments prove that a text can be dated or "localized" without knowing the writer: by analysis of the hand-writing, of the structure of the sentence, of the use of parts of speech, of the type of subject, of the metaphors and, generally, of the overall esthetic demands of a milieu which we will call here "conventions."[6] Whatever the creative genius of a writer, while he may infringe upon the demands of his public's taste, he cannot be unaware of it.

The interlacing of styles (*précieux*, baroque, burlesque, grotesque, classical) in seventeenth century France would doubtless be better understood if the possible public at the origin of each one of them could be perceived more clearly. Men are not too different culturally, linguistically or in their ideas, but they make up groups, cliques and teams, each of which has its own atmosphere, its style and, moreover, its own esthetic. Corneille, the provincial, was plunged into that rough bourgeoisie which comes out of religious wars burning with action, heroism and will power. La Calprenède also wrote for this bourgeoisie in a genre which perhaps suited it better than tragedy: the novel. It is natural that Corneille's Parisian success led him to strike out without understanding at the incomprehension of an Academy of men who were not unlike him but who symbolized the new Parisian orthodoxy of the *bel esprit* and who were busy formulating a society in which Corneille was a stranger, the esthetic of another generation, the one we now call classical. Therefore the quarrel of the *Cid* was a dialogue between deaf-mutes much like the quarrel between the Ancients and the Moderns sixty years later, and for identical reasons.

If we wish to connect these few, minutely adumbrative explanations with what we discovered statistically in Chapter Three— the blockade of a literary population by an in-

5. Thierry Maulnier, *Racine* (1935), pp. 42-43.
6. On "conventions," see B. Muntéano, "Des 'constantes' en littérature," *Revue de littérature comparée*, XXXI (July - September 1957), 388-420.

cumbent group, the succession of generations— and in Chapter Four— the Paris-province exchange, the variations of social milieux— we will understand that these phenomena demonstrate the action of the milieu-public on the vocation and the meaning of writers.

Nevertheless we have but a part of the total picture; the study of the public indigenous to the writer's milieu, its culture, its language, its literary genres and its style, does not, by itself, account for the entire literary fact. Actually, beyond geographic, chronological and social boundaries, an immense public exists which cannot impose on the writer any determinants, but in which a work may best continue its life through reading, most often through word-of-mouth or through some unpredictable metamorphosis. For cultured writers the popular circuit public, now called the "public-at-large," belongs to this *terra incognita* in which can also be found the foreign public and the future public known as posterity. Many are those writers who, suffocating in cells too restricted for them, have taken these unsuspected masses for their own public and have written their work for them, reflecting their idea of that public: they have been tempted to write populist or cosmopolitan literature, or to write for posterity. But only a few writers have received a response in this hypothetical dialogue.

And even so, the response is distorted. Alien publics cannot penetrate a work with the same detachment and ease that familiarity gives to the writer's original social group. Incapable of perceiving objectively the reality of the literary fact, they substitute subjective myths for it. Most classifications in literary history for a critic who does not know how to limit them strictly to their function as working hypotheses are only myths of this kind. They are invented by a posterity that has become estranged from the realities which they replace: uses made of such terms as *humanistic, classical, picaresque, burlesque*, or *romantic*, often have no more real significance nowadays than our common use of the term *existentialist*. Sometimes the myth is personal and presupposes eponymous heroes: the hero of Corneille, Goethe or Balzac; in 1958, similarly, thousands in France referred to "Saganism" (so phonetically close to Satanism) without having ever opened a book by Françoise Sagan.

Byron was one of the rare authors who, before the movie era (the myth-sustaining technique above all others) became legendary in his lifetime. Few men have given birth to so many myths, from that of the dark stranger of the school-boys in 1815 to that of the militant revolutionary which presently has currency in the USSR, and let us not forget his apotheosis as the club-footed devil in Victorian society About 1820, exile allowed him to see the rise of his romantic myth, but he was already a prisoner of it by then. From the time in 1812 when *Childe Harold* and then the *Giaour* in 1813 broke through the equivalent of what we have called the "100,000 wall," the myth took root in places alien to his social group, in that "suburban reader" whom he disdained. Byron, although only half-conscious of it, fed his myth by yielding to the temptation of power which large editions provide. In fact, the myth intervened between himself and the public-at-large as if it were a mirror reflecting to that public its own image. The day came when the mirror lost its silvering and another Byron appeared, unintelligible and inaccessible to many (that of *Don Juan*, which is unanimously preferred by cultured readers). Then the "witchhunt" was unleashed, for one does not do violence with impunity to the integrity of a myth, even if one has given life to it himself.[7]

We previously stated that the public-at-large has no influence on a writer. This is not quite exact. It has each time a writer surrenders himself to it by committing the cardinal literary sin: accepting success which is not his but that of a myth. Inevitably this imposture is later paid for because the public which has made use of the myth to gain access to a work has not drawn purely literary pleasure from it: the public has used it. Such is the drama of a Kipling, buried beneath the imperialistic myth.[8]

Success

The diverse publics which we have so far envisaged (the addressed public, the public of communal assumptions, the public-at-large) cannot serve as a yardstick for commercial success, for they are only theoretical. Commercially, the only real public is that constituted of book buyers. In this sense it can be said that there are four degrees of success: failure, when the sale of a book shows a deficit for both publisher and bookseller; half-success, when the sales of a book balance its budget; average success, when sales approximately equal the publisher's prediction; the best seller, when sales outstrip foreseeable limits and escape control.

The triggering of success, notably that of the best seller, remains an unpredictable and inexplicable phenomenon. But it is now undoubtedly possible to shed light on the great mechanical laws of success after it has been set in motion. The data we have are still too fragmentary for us to attach much importance to them: publishers and booksellers are

---

7. See R. Escarpit, *Lord Byron, un tempérament littéraire*, I (1957), 111-117 and 179-184.

8. We defended this point of view in our study, *Rudyard Kipling, servitudes et grandeurs impériales* (1955).

either too reticent or too primitively organized to furnish the indispensable information. But sooner or later, serious research will have to take place in this domain.[9]

This kind of research will have to include particularly the organization of diagrams of distribution by regions, social levels, etc., assuming a sufficient sampling of titles. This information will be compared with the diverse factors which influence the general behavior of the public.

Commercial success, however, granted its importance for the life of a book, can be considered only as an indication that needs interpretation. The reality of literary success lies elsewhere, for, at the risk of being repetitive, a book is not simply a material object. From the author's point of view, in a sense, success begins with the first buyer or even the first anonymous reader for, through him, as we have seen, literary creation is fulfilled.

We said at the beginning of this study that there can be no literature without a convergence of intentions between author and reader or at the very least a compatibility of intention. It is time now to elucidate these two ideas. There may be such a distance between what the author wishes to express in his work and what the reader hopes to find that no contact is possible. The reader's sole recourse then is to interpose between himself and the writer that mirror, which we have called myth, which is provided by his social group. European publics have come to "know" most Far-Eastern writers in such a way.

But when writer and reader belong to the same social group, the intentions of both may coincide. It is in this coincidence that literary success lies. In other words, the successful book is one which expresses that which its public expects, which reveals the public to itself. The impressions of having shared the same ideas, the same feelings, of having lived the same vicissitudes, are those most frequently mentioned by readers of a successful book.

Thus it may be said that the extent of a writer's success within his group is proportionate to his aptitude to be the "resounding echo" of which Victor Hugo speaks, and that the number of copies sold and the duration of a book's success depend on the dimensions of the public in the writer's milieu.

As a matter of fact, these dimensions are quite variable. Certain writers belong to minorities or to periods of short

9. One of the rare studies of this type has been carried out by J. Hassen-Forder with the help of the Seuil Publishing Company. He has stated his results in a work mimeographed by the Centre D'Etudes Economiques: *Etude de la diffusion d'un succès de librairie* (Paris, 1957).

duration.[10] Others are sustained by vast social groups, classes or nations, or even by chronological communities which spread over several generations.

The illusion of the universality or of the perenniality of a writer can be explained in such a fashion. "Universal" or "eternal" writers are those whose collective position in literature is particularly spread out in time or space, who seek farther their contemporaries or their "tribal" brothers. Molière is still young for the French in the twentieth century because his world still lives; we still have in common with him culture, concepts and language. His plays continue to be produced because his irony is still attainable to us, but the circle is shrinking and Molière will grow older and will die when that part of French civilization which has something in common with Molière's France dies.

The illusion of the underrated genius can also be explained in this way. Certain writers are chronologically "remote" in relation to their group. For the most part we are not talking about "latecomers," because we do not have the opportunity of knowing that they have been underrated. Forerunners, however, see their success amplified and multiplied, often in several generations' time when the minority which supported them originally becomes developed and takes on importance and influence. The example of Lou Sin, to which we referred above, is that of most of the Marxist writers before the Soviet Revolution. But on a less grandiose scale, the same diagram could apply to Stendhal or to the *poètes maudits* of the nineteenth century. In any case, there must have occurred first a success, a birth, however modest, maintained by the same social group without interruption from one generation to another. Without this, the writer dies, and that kind of death is permanent.

We should not confuse this variable extent of original success with resuscitations or resurrections which enable a work to find beyond social, spatial or temporal obstacles substitute success in groups foreign to the writer's own public. We have seen that alien publics do not have direct access to the work. What they ask of the work is not what its author wishes to express. There is no coincidence or convergence of intention, but there may be compatibility; that is, they may find what they want in the work although the author did not expressly or perhaps even consciously put it there.

We are dealing here with treason, certainly, but it is creative treason. The irritating problem of translating would perhaps be resolved if we admitted that it is always an act

---

10. We must insist that this fact takes nothing away from the intrinsic and local value of the work. Bourget, Proust and Gide died with their world, but they nonetheless remain as historical values.

of creative treason, but it is still treason because it puts the work into a system of references (linguistic, in this example) for which it was not originally conceived— creative because it gives new reality to the work in providing it with the possibility of a new literary interchange with a larger public and because it assures not only mere survival but a second existence.[11] Practically all of ancient and medieval literature lives today only through creative treason, the origins of which stem from the sixteenth century and which have been renewed several times since that century.

Two of the most characteristic examples of creative treason are *Gulliver's Travels* by Swift and *Robinson Crusoe* by Defoe. The first of these books was originally a cruel satire of such black humor that it would relegate Jean-Paul Sartre to the optimism of the *Bibliothèque Rose*. The second is a sermon (often tedious) on the glory of budding colonialism. Now these books survive today, enjoying in fact unfailing success, through their integration with children's literature! They have become Christmas presents. Defoe would have been amused by it, Swift enraged, but both would have been greatly surprised. Nothing could have been more alien to their intentions. Marvelous and exotic adventures constitute the essential quality that young readers seek in these works, but they were only a banal technique for their authors, a popular genre in their society, constructed after much research and borrowed from Hakluyt, Mandeville and other travel-adventure writers. The real message is now only intelligible by means of an interpretation the modern reader is unable to make. Thus he contents himself with the form (adapted, it is true) which remains the one accessible to him at the beginning of adolescence. All this brings to mind the famous story of the madman who threw out the liquid and ate the glass: this, in a sense, was also creative treason!

These acts of treason take place not only from era to era but from country to country, and even from social group to social group within one country. Kipling, who was killed in England by the imperialist myth, was reborn in France before his physical death in the domain of children's literature and in the USSR in militant literature. Kipling meditated

---

11. The Russian formalists have defended an apparently analagous point of view: "Consequently, the literature of translations must be studied as a component element of the literature of each nation. In addition to a French Béranger and a German Heine, there existed a Russian Béranger and Russian Heine who satisfied the needs of Russian literature and who, doubtless, were rather far removed from their Western homonyms." ("La nouvelle école d'histoire littéraire en Russie," *Revue des Études slaves,* VIII (1928), 226-240). This extreme position is not ours: the French Béranger and the Russian Béranger construct the literary and historical Béranger who was already present (unconsciously) in the work of Béranger.

much on Swift's example and the unwarranted gifts of literary Providence which withheld the success he had earned but gave him triumphs he had never dreamed of. Towards the end of his life, in a talk before the *Royal Society of Literature,* he affirmed the writer's inability to foresee what truths his work would engender beyond the limits of its universe.

Perhaps its susceptibility to betrayal is the mark of the *great* literary work. This idea is not impossible, but it is not certain. What is certain, however, is that the true face of a literary work is revealed, sculptured and deformed by the various uses which its public makes of it. To know what a book is presupposes a knowledge of how it has been read.[12]

---

12. George H. Ford, in *Dickens and his Readers* (Princeton, 1955), gives a good example of criticism which takes into account the reader's influence. See also our article, " 'Creative Treason' as a Key to Literature," *Yearbook of Comparative and General Literature,* No. X, 1961.

CHAPTER VIII

Reading and Life

Connoisseurs and Consumers

THE DISTANCE which separates textbook literature from living literature is a traditional subject of jokes or scandal. It seems absurd to "lose" several years of one's existence studying wearisome texts which will never be reread. This view confuses the aptitudes of the connoisseur with those of the consumer. The characteristic of the cultured person is his theoretical capacity to make justifiable literary judgments. High school training aims at making this kind of judgment possible and, especially in France, the pedagogical technique of the *explication de texte*, the pillar of secondary education, tends to make a connoisseur of each reader.

Unfortunately, the act of reading is not just an act of informing oneself. It is an experience which involves the entire human being— both his individual and collective aspects. The reader is a consumer and, like all consumers, he is guided by taste and does not really exercise a judgment, even if he is capable of rationally justifying his taste *a posteriori.*

Since the exercise of literary judgment is the characteristic of the cultured group (which itself is often assimilated into a caste or a social class as high-school graduates used to be in France), this group makes its members act like connoisseurs under the threat of moral sanctions, such as being labeled a crude individual, a Philistine, even a "primitive." Such is the mechanism of censure that we pointed out above and which makes investigations of reading habits so difficult: how would a cultured man whose judgment enables him to appreciate the value of a play by Racine dare admit that his taste leads him to prefer reading the comic strip, *Tintin?*[1] People under pressure from their social and cultural group are forced to indicate their taste in the form of

---

1. This is said without any pejorative intentions towards Hervé, who (and we are betraying no secret here) is in great favor among the faculty in the universities. His work was quoted five times during a recent meeting of literary historians.

justifiable arguments. So they have recourse to myths ending in "ism" which provide them with ready-made rational justifications.

This confusion would undoubtedly be avoided if we clearly recognized two entirely distinct orders of value in the justified arguments of the connoisseur and the irrational taste of the consumer.

The role of the connoisseur is to "go beyond appearances," to perceive the circumstances which surround literary creation, to understand its intentions, to analyze its means. For him, there is no such thing as aging or death of a work, as it is possible at any given moment to reconstruct in his mind the system of references which restores to any work its esthetic nature. This is an historical attitude.

The consumer, on the contrary, lives in the present, albeit the present may have its origins in a rather distant past. He has no active role, merely an existence. He tastes what is offered him and decides whether or not it pleases him. The decision has no need of being explicit: the consumer reads or doesn't read. This attitude in no way excludes intellectual lucidity on his part, nor does it rule out someone's examination of the reasons for his preference which demands more perspicacity than simply justifying it.

The two orders of value can and must coexist; sometimes they even coincide. Their apparent incompatibility is only an effect of the social and cultural structures which we have described and, in particular, of the isolation of the cultured circuit. In fact, whatever the patterns of the reader's intellectual and emotional reaction, the act of reading is a whole and must be considered as an entity. Like the act of literary creation which is at the other end of the chain, it is a free act influenced by the circumstances within which it occurs. Its profound nature is, at least for the moment, impenetrable to scrutiny, but we can hunt it down by interpreting the behavior of the various categories of readers, not in relation to a literary judgment, but in relation to a situation.

We have only fragmentary information on this behavior and most of it is based on observations of librarians and cultural leaders. It is still quite an insufficient source from which to draw conclusions, but the example of women's reading demonstrates the kind of information one could obtain from a systematic investigation.

On all levels of society, the behavior of women readers seems more homogeneous that that of male readers. What we commonly call escape literature— we shall soon qualify this term— is relatively frequent (sentimental, historical and detective novels); just as often in the cultured circuit as in the popular one, female writers are among the favorites (around 1955, Pearl Buck, Daphne du Maurier, Mazo de la Roche, Colette and especially, eternally, Delly). To this list may be added other writers who confirm the tendency towards "escape" in their works (Loti, Pierre Benoît, Paul Vialar, etc.), as well as a few who interpret the world of daily preoccupations (Van der Meersch, Cronin, Slaughter, Thyde Monnier, Soubiran, etc.).

This homogeneity is evidently due to the fact that women's way of life is relatively uniform, especially today: household chores and children most often added to a professional activity cut women's lives along patterns analagous at all social levels and in all geographical regions. As to the particular kind of reading they choose, it goes back to the seventeenth and eighteenth centuries. Boredom, at a time when the social and political responsibilities of women were practically non-existent, was undoubtedly one of the sources of the romantic novel. Writers such as Pearl Buck or A. J. Cronin express new preoccupations, which will no doubt have an ever-growing influence as the status of women progresses towards a greater participation in civic life.

Let us also note that escape literature seems most frequently chosen by young women (between 30 and 40) on whom *bovaryism* has a stronger hold. Generally, the older a person becomes the more literary his reading— and this is true both of men and women. The retired person is often a reader of books of excellent quality, probably because he has more time to read, but also because life exerts less pressure on him.

Consequently, we should study the psychological motivations and the material circumstances which condition the behavior of the common reader.[2]

Motivation

We know that the purchase of a book is not to be confused with its reading. It can happen that a person buys (or, more rarely, borrows) a book without having any particular intention of reading it, even if he does read it eventually.

We can cite the "ostentatious" acquisition of a book that one "just has to have" as a sign of wealth, culture or good taste (this is one of the status symbols most frequently

2. See the admirable study of Richard D. Altick, *The English Common Reader. A Social History of the Mass Reading Public, 1800-1900* (Chicago, 1957), and, although less precise, that of R. K. Webb, *The British Working Class Reader, 1790-1848* (London, 1955).

played upon by French book clubs): the investment of money in rare books, the habitual purchase of volumes of a certain series, the purchase of a book through fidelity to a cause or person (success based on admiration) or the purchase of a book because it is beautiful— in this instance the book is then appreciated as an *objet d'art*, for its binding, its typography or its illustrations.

Consumption without reading interests us only in so far as it is a part of the economic cycle of the book. However, it represents only a minute fraction of total consumption, especially in popular circuits where, although one often buys a newspaper intending to read only part of it, he rarely purchases a book without the intention of reading it.

We also know when dealing with the consumption-reading of a book that we have to distinguish between utilitarian consumption and literary consumption, and that different kinds of motivation correspond to each.

We will touch upon functional motivations only briefly. First, there are news, documentary information and professional studies. More complex than these is the functional use of the literary book. One of the most characteristic is a therapeutic use when the book plays a medicinal role, when, for example, one reads to go to sleep or to occupy one's mind and to turn it away physically from anxiety. Similarly, there is "reading for relaxation" that makes the mind undergo mental gymnastics: a certain type of detective novel is analagous in this respect to a crossword puzzle. In other instances, the reader may expect the book to serve as a drug directly on the nervous system in order to obtain certain sensations. Some examples are horror literature, hilarious literature (appealing to a mechanical comic reaction), tear-provoking literature and especially erotic literature. Let us point out, speaking of the latter, that the erotic use of literature is a very frequent motivation for reading, even if the pornographic aspects are but minor elements in the book or are not even consciously introduced into the work.

Although on quite another level, we should also consider as functional, or at least partly functional, the reading of militants or of autodidacts. For them the book serves as the instrument of combat techniques or of social promotion. Thus, the book may be read in order to acquire culture, not primarily to enjoy reading: literary motivations may exist, but they are secondary.

Real literary motivations respect the gratuitousness of the work and do not use the work as a means, but rather as an end. Thus conceived, reading implies solitude even as it excludes solitude. In fact, to read a book as an original creation and not as a tool destined to satisfy a need presupposes that we *go to another person*, that we *have recourse to someone else*, and thus, that we get away from ourselves for a time. In this sense, the companion-book is opposed to the utensil-book which is completely subordinated to the demands of the individual. Nevertheless, reading is the supreme solitary occupation. The man who reads does not speak, does not act, cuts himself away from society, isolates himself from the world which surrounds him. This is as true of "auditive reading" as it is of visual reading. No one is more isolated from his fellow man than the spectator in a theatre. Let us note here a fundamental difference between literature and the fine arts: while music and painting can serve as settings, even as functional frameworks, for our activities because they involve only part of our attention, reading allows the senses no margin of liberty. It absorbs the entire conscious mind, making the reader powerless to act.

The act of reading is thus at the same time social and asocial. It temporarily suppresses the individual's relations with his universe to construct new ones with the universe of the work. Consequently, the motivation to read is almost always dissatisfaction, a lack of harmony between the reader and his milieu, whether due to causes inherent in human nature (shortness and frailty of existence) or to the clash of individuals (love, hate, pity), or to social structures (oppression, poverty, fear of the future, boredom). In a word, it is a recourse against the absurdity of the human condition. A happy people might not have a history, but it certainly would have no literature for it would not feel the need to read.

The term "escape literature" has been used frequently without perhaps having been clearly defined. The nuance of disdain or defiance that people most often cast upon it is rather an arbitrary one. All reading in truth is primarily an escape. But there are a thousand ways to escape and it is essential to know from what and towards what we are escaping. The study of reading in relation to political events, notably in periods of stress such as wars, international crises, revolutions, etc., would be most revealing in this respect.

The success of *Don Camillo* has been particularly great in countries where profound political divisions exist. The spectacle of a rugged friendship that did not permit betrayal existing between a communist and a priest, both deeply entrenched in the soil, while it did not obliterate divisions, checked their harmful power and made them tolerable. The euphoria which surrounded the beginning of the Mendès-France experiment in 1954 was one of the elements which spurred the success of the *Notebooks of Major Thompson*, not because that euphoria created a demand for light readings, but, on the contrary, because it was trying to sustain itself, to overcome its frailty by reasserting the great commonplace characteristics of the national soul (particularly effective in a foreigner's mouth). Then in December of 1956, during the week of the Suez crisis just at the moment when *Notebooks* lost its effectiveness and really became escape literature, the sale of that book, which had remained at a high rate for two years, suddenly slipped at the rate of ten to two.

We are grateful to Mr. Jean Dulck of the University of Bordeaux for a diagram of the plays performed in London at the end of the eighteenth century. The war against France broke out in April, 1792. Now the number of farces performed were nine in 1791 and ten in 1792. In 1793 only one farce was presented. At the same time, the number of *comédies de moeurs* went from four in 1792 to six in 1793, and to twelve in 1795. Tragedies increased from three in 1792 to five in 1793 and to ten in 1794 and 1795. As supply is extremely sensitive to demand in the theatre (especially at that time), we may consider these variations as excellent examples of the influence exercised by crises on literary consumption— not necessarily in the direction we call escape. Farce is, by nature, an infinitely less "involved" genre than the *comédie de moeurs* or tragedy.

We lack data to continue beyond this point, but when a sufficient quantity of data is collected, there will be a vast terrain that social psychology will have to clear. Let us just say that we must avoid confusing the escape of a prisoner (a conquest, an enriching experience), with that of a deserter (a defeat, an impoverishing experience). Let us note moreover that motivations cannot be judged according to what one reads. The enrichment the reader demands from a work —to reconcile himself with the absurdity of the human condition, to return to emotional stability, to acquire the language of self-consciousness— can be, as we have said elsewhere, "paid for either in a kind of solid currency immediately convertible into experience, or in 'fool's gold'— useless checks drawn on illusions."[3]

Our knowledge of distributing reading materials allows us to affirm that in countries not applying a policy of literary dictatorship, the majority of reading materials distributed in the cultured circuit presupposes (if only as an alibi) a motivation of desertion. From the hawker's pouch to the bookstore shelf, an entire stereotyped literature seeks to flatter the public-at-large through the crude sentimental mythology of latent *bovaryism* which has so often been cultivated in the masses.

These comparisons are arbitrary. They do not specify any reality about attitudes. They simply demonstrate a

---

3. "Les lectures populaires, *"Informations sociales* (February 1956), p. 202.

factual state, an established situation, or an economic-social structure. Whatever motivations make us read, they can be effective only in favorable material circumstances.

The Circumstances of Reading

We shall not repeat what we have said about distribution. But new problems are raised, once we have assumed that a book is available to a reader. Where and when can one read?

To answer this question, we must first examine the idea of availability. Life in society absorbs an individual in various ways. Thus one's age is an important factor. Education, vocational training and job-hunting leave adolescents and young men such little spare time for non-functional reading that that spare time is usually devoted to numerous other distractions, particularly sports. The young person reads just the same, for his motivations are powerful (this is the age of personality crises and of collision with society). Such a reader is avid and passionate, but all polls indicate that he reads little outside of his studies and that the circle of his reading is relatively narrow. It is between thirty-five and forty, when the pressure of existence makes itself less actively felt, that the reading age seems to begin. It will be remembered that it is also at this age that the historical, literary personality of writers is fixed. Perhaps a rapport exists between these two facts; only a really effective examination of the problem would enable us to state that it does in fact exist.

Among other factors which affect availability, the reader's kind of work must be mentioned as well as his home, climatic conditions, family situation, etc. Each will have to be studied in detail, but already we know that generally there are three great categories of available time in man's life today: those unrecoverable slack moments (traveling, eating, etc.), regular free time (after the day's work), periods of non-activity (Sunday, holidays, illness, retirement).

Reading in the first category is devoted mostly to newspapers. The irregularity and brevity of those periods, along with frequent interruptions and other diversions, make continued reading difficult. However, while the reading one does at meals is nearly always in a newspaper, reading materials for traveling or commuting are specialized: for example, novels "to be read on the train," mainly detective novels. But ordinary novels are adapted to rather long distances (two or three hours of reading) and so are rarely suited to the worker's daily trip to and from his place of employment. One of the success factors of digests is that they offer reading in doses. Sentimental novels, especially conceived for this purpose, take the form of brochures of sixteen, thirty-two, sixty-four or ninety-six pages, corresponding to trips of ten minutes to an hour. One solution used in Great Britain is that of large digests which carry a reservoir of reading materials for several weeks, but their bulk usually makes them impractical.

Coffee breaks may be assimilated into the slack moment category. Reading at this time is rare, for conversation, discussions and the *bistro* provide unbeatable competition. However, experience proves that if favorable material conditions are furnished on the spot— i.e., a club room, a library—even the coffee break can allow for active and fruitful reading.

Reading in free time is most frequent by far. There are two kinds: reading in the evening, in general with the family, before or immediately after the evening meal, and reading at night, most often in bed. Reading in the evening is done especially by older persons less tempted by external amusements. It is favored by rustic life (long evenings at home), by intemperate climates (evening reading is practically nonexistent in Mediterranean countries, although greatly practiced in Great Britain and the Scandinavian countries) and by the comfort of home. Radio and especially television tend to substitute "audio-visual reading" for the visual reading of a book. Audio-visual reading is not without merit but implies a control on reading matter. Nonetheless, the most solid reading is still done in the evening.

Reading at night has its own peculiar traits; readers who are interviewed mention that kind of reading most willingly. For quite some time the importance of the bedside book (that is, the one kept on the nightstand), has been recognized. In fact, it reflects the reader's tastes most exactly, for in the solitude of the bedroom taboos lose their potency and social constraints are eliminated. It would be extremely important to conduct a particular study of the bedside book, for more time is devoted to this sort of reading than to any other, often two or more hours every night.

As for reading in non-active periods, it has very diverse aspects. We have already said a few words about reading during retirement. Reading on Sunday must compete with hobbies and sports. It often takes the form of the Sunday newspaper: in Great Britain, 23.5% of the adult population read three or more Sunday newspapers!

Reading during illness is, fortunately, unusual, but it is not any less effective. Long hours in bed allow for reading in depth which many readers will never again have the opportunity to do. This observation is especially true of convalescence, as illness itself puts up better with functional reading. Here, too, everything depends on the material facilities available. Hospital libraries in France are lamentably under-stocked. It is there, however, that one's most important and decisive readings may occur.

We know little about reading on vacations. It has num-erous competitors, but it does exist nonetheless on beaches, in the outdoors and in spas. We have personally studied a little city on the seaside to which from 10,000 to 15,000 vacationers flock each summer. It has one bookstore and three other sources of book sales. In the bookstore and in one of the other stores (which also sells daily newspapers), the most recent novels are found. Apparently few books remain unsold (although both establishments can return them to the publishing houses). There are two commercial lending libraries and a parish lending library. The main lend-ing library (affiliated with the bookstore) carries about three thousand volumes (about three hundred of them detective novels). The rest of the stock is made up of French or foreign novels (sixty per cent) and documentaries, historical and ad-venture books. In addition there are a few didactic and philosophical works. At the height of the season, up to eight hundred readers are registered and the turnover is very rapid (one volume every two days on the average). A fraction of the clientele specializes in detective novels. In the other cate-gories there is a waiting list for recent novels and travel books.

This analysis is, of course, only an adumbration, but the example of the *Notebooks of Major Thompson* shows how in-teresting it would be to duplicate and develop it. The book was published in May, that is, too late to be distributed according to publication custom. It owed the rapidity of its initial sales pace in part to readers at seaside resorts. The beginning of the summer was rainy and thus created a vast demand— and this book was practically the only "novelty" offered in bookstores at that time of year.

These all too brief indications show to what extent reading is linked to circumstance and is generally an integral part of daily life. There, in the humble reality of everyday life, the goal and justification of all literature are to be found. Thus we cannot fail to be struck by the disproportion which exists between this reality and the social apparatus of litera-ture such as we have described it. With such a disproportion, is literature still a vital part of society? That will be our last question.

Conclusion

In concluding this study at this point, we are aware of its incomplete schematic nature. But the objections which it will provoke will undoubtedly bear less on the presented

95

facts than on the spirit which animates it. After so much sociology and pseudo-sociology, one will say, what remains of literature? Aren't we precondemning literature by defining it as a gratuitous fact?

We accept the objection but answer that literature is taken here for what it is and not for what it should be. We have not tried to hide that literature's place in contemporary society is far from satisfactory. It is possible that this society no longer admits gratuitousness or at least no longer admits the kind of gratuitousness of which a cultured contemporary of Madame de Staël could conceive.

The concept of literature that we use, by means of which we give shape to the literary fact, is therefore badly adapted to our times. Born in the eighteenth century under the pressure of circumstances— the accession of the middle class to literary culture, the industrialization of the bookstore, the appearance of the professional man of letters— this concept can possibly give us an intelligible if still deformed image of former centuries by virtue of an act of "creative treason." But it is less and less capable of enclosing the present within its narrow limits. Just about everywhere, the culture of the masses is beginning to appear, to make demands which cannot always be expressed by language or realized by institutions; but it increases its pressures from day to day. Methods of distribution, even more powerful because they are not in the hands of small enterprises, are growing with book manufacturing and sales: these methods include not only the movies, radio and television, but also the press and periodicals with their cartoons and digests. Patronage having been absorbed by authoritarian controls and the old structures of literary publication being insufficient to support the writer, the writer then finds himself isolated and relegated to the indefinable category of "intellectual," in between the liberal professions and the salaried worker.

The word matters little: "literature" is as good as any other. What we must find is a new equilibrium. The one which we inherited from the eighteenth century is shaken. Only an effort at lucidity will make us take stock of the equilibrium being created around us, often without our knowledge.

To accomplish this, literature must be brought down from its pedestal and disencumbered from its social taboos; the secret of their strength must be unveiled. Then perhaps, it will be possible to retrace not the history of literature, but the history of man in society by examining the dialogue of the creators of words, myth and ideas with their contemporaries and their posterity, the dialogue that we now call literature.

APPENDIX

The Age Factor in Literary Productivity

Translated from *Bulletin des Bibliothèques de France*, V
(May 1960), 105-111.

In my short study, *Sociology of Literature*, I make reference to an experiment undertaken by the American psychologist Harvey C. Lehman concerning the age at which authors wrote certain literary works.[1] Let us briefly describe the nature of this experiment.

First, Lehman had Asa Don Dickinson, former librarian of the University of California, establish a list of "best books." This list was obtained by cross-checking fifty lists which themselves were made from polls of the cultured milieu in the United States. The choice of books included in the list could be varied from Grade 1, Grade 2, Grade 3 and so on to Grade 50, that is, books mentioned one, two, three and up to fifty times in the combined lists. Thus Grade I included all the books while Grade 50 had only a small number. In general, Lehman worked on the selection of books from Grade 8.

The experiment to which I am alluding is the following. In a list of 733 "best books" by 488 authors, Lehman separated authors living at the time of the establishment of the list from those who had died by that time. There were 203 deceased authors and they had written 337 books. There were 285 living authors with 396 works. Next, Lehman found out at what age the author wrote each of the considered works; then having separated each category (dead and living) by age groups, he made the following corresponding curves:

Age	Dead	Alive	Age	Dead	Alive
20-24	7	0	55-59	29	52
25-29	24	18	60-64	38	43
30-34	37	29	65-69	17	59
35-39	63	60	70-74	13	58
40-44	55	68	75-79	20	21
45-49	56	62	80-84	18	0
50-54	42	55	85+	(57)	0

(The variation in the last age group can be considered negligible since so few works are represented).

1. Harvey C. Lehman, "The Creative Years: 'Best Books,'" *The Scientific Monthly*, VL (July 1937), 65-75.

97

The graph below reveals a "zone of oblivion" which demonstrates that after the authors' deaths one forgets especially works written after 40, while one particularly remembers works written about the age of 40.

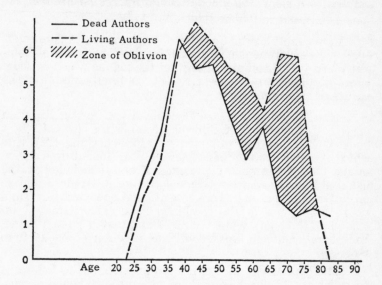

Having worked on lists of various grades, Lehman shows that in proportion as the list diminishes, works of dead authors fall rapidly into oblivion after age 40.

He draws the following conclusion: 40 is, on the average, the age of maximum output, of the "best book." Moreover, he believes he can corroborate this statement by studying the age at which authors wrote works on "masterpiece" lists (established by polls) or of best sellers. He even goes to the extent of comparing—for 152 German authors—quantitative output (works actually published) with qualitative output (works chosen by polls). He obtains a graph table analagous to the one representing the comparison of live and dead authors.

Convinced that 40 years is the best age for writing, Lehman continued his research by comparing the effect of the age factor on yield in diverse intellectual and physical activities.[2] He compared particularly athletics with movies and

2. Harvey C. Lehman, "'Intellectual' Versus 'Physical' Peak Performance: the Age Factor," *The Scientific Monthly*, LXIX (August 1945), 127-137.

scientific discoveries, science with music, philosophy with literature, billiards and golf with oil painting, target shooting and fertility with poetry, chemistry with billiards, football with lyric poetry, etc. Although we may sometimes be tempted to smile at the incongruity of some of these associations, we cannot fail to be struck by certain coincidences. It is interesting to note, for example, that lyric poetry has a curve equal to physical activity, which demands great precision and quick reflexes. This activity is mainly practiced by young people: the culminating point is between twenty-five and thirty.

Having said so much, it appears to us that Lehman is on the wrong road. Without denying that the years between thirty-five and forty, which are probably those where intellectual maturity and physical capacity are almost perfectly balanced, are those of the best yield, the acknowledged milestone of age forty can, indeed, have another meaning. We must not forget that we are not born in a biological sense to literature, but rather in a social sense. The latter event takes place at varying ages when the author is recognized as such by his social group.

An easy and amusing experiment will prove our point: that of writers' longevity. We know that a normal longevity curve climbs very slowly until it reaches forty years, accelerates its climb until around seventy, where it begins a bell whose apex is around seventy-five or eighty years, when most deaths occur. Then the curve descends rapidly through extinction of the samples.

If we now try to establish this curve for any sample of writers, we shall obtain a quite normal curve whose summit, however, is slightly shifted towards the left; that is, it will be somewhat "younger." Then let us isolate the different literary genres and set up separate curves for poets, playwrights, novelists, philosophers, historians, etc. We will notice the following facts:

a) The curve of novelists is normal until the 70-75 year summit, then descends much more quickly than the normal curve.

b) The curve of poets climbs abnormally quickly, with subsidiary summits between 30 and 50; it attains a "young" summit around 65 years, then descends abnormally slowly.

c) The curve of playwrights is normal, from one end to the other, but it is entirely shifted from ten to fifteen years towards youth.

d) The curve of historians and philosophers is also normal, but it is entirely shifted towards old age by five to ten years.

Of course, we must be careful not to conclude from this that the theatre kills, that philosophy and history preserve life, that the novel is fatal to old men and that poetry, that contradictory elixir, strikes down certain temperaments while prolonging the lives of others. The only legitimate way in which to interpret the more or less large number of deaths in a given type of writer at a given age is to say that, among persons deceased at that age, a more or less large number were famous enough to be recognized by the public as writers in their respective specialities. Thus the only statement we can make about this study on lifespan is the fact that a playwright may come of literary age relatively early, a philosopher or a historian relatively late, that one can become a poet at any age and that a man, as he grows older, has less and less chance to become a novelist. The variations of the longevity curve show us only— and only approximately—variations in the age at which a writer becomes recognized as such, the age of his literary birth. Now this birth into literature, even supposing individual aptitudes, is above all a social birth (and in this sense, Lehman is not altogether wrong); it is the result of the public's perception.

It will be interesting to determine the average age of literary birth. There is data on the subject which has not as yet been established scientifically, but various surveys lead us to think that the immense majority of writers are born to literature between twenty-five and thirty; that is, they achieve at that age the decisive success that makes them writers in the public's eyes. That public will then follow their careers, embrace them in the dialogue which inevitably occurs between author and reader, will occasionally wear them out. Now it is rare that one generation's dialogues are similar to those of the preceding generation. After a certain time, a new generation of readers reaches maturity and its taste invades newspapers and publishing houses, with repercussions on the bookstore trade and, in a more vague fashion, on the buying policy of libraries. The authors who were popular up to that time lose their echo little by little, and finally enter a period of deafness, if not oblivion. This crisis may be final if the author dies or ceases to produce for such a period of time that he cannot keep his appointment with the next generation. But if he does continue to produce, chances are that some day he will find his echo once more and that his works will become important again. This is really a periodic phenomenon which goes on long after the author's death. It can be easily discerned if we look at Lehman's diagram in Figure 1. We notice that the importance of the "zone of oblivion" is not constant. It begins between age thirty-five and forty, but is marked by a first constriction between forty-five and fifty, then a second one between sixty and sixty-five and a third and final one between seventy-five and eighty. At each constriction, the works of dead authors tend to revert to the level of living authors' works as if there were a decrease in the period of oblivion. Conversely, between each constriction, there is the sign of a crisis. This periodicity occurs clearly every fifteen years.

Given these conditions, it is easy to understand why Lehman observes that forty is always a decisive age. It occurs from ten to fifteen years (or one period of the cycle) after the average age of initial success, of literary birth. It is the age of the second chance after which the first crisis of oblivion, the first sorting, the first reckoning will begin.

Age forty does not signify, then, a culminating point in the absolute productivity of writers, but at that age questions of permanence begin to be posed. Let us emphasize that we are dealing with an average age which corresponds to an average age of success. If an author becomes famous before or after the 25-30 age period, his summit will be shifted accordingly.

A final experiment, an unprecedented one, will allow us to state precisely the meaning of the age of forty and its influence on productivity.

In a remarkable study of the book industry in France at the time of the *ancien régime*, David T. Pottinger has studied the literary production of a sampling of writers.[3] To

---

3. *The French Book Trade in the Ancient Regime, 1550-1791* (Cambridge, Massachusetts, 1958).

establish his sample, Pottinger initiated a cross-checking of lists published in the eighteenth century, using a method analagous to Lehman's but adapted to a historical perspective. However, he committed the serious statistical error of selecting 200 authors born in the sixteenth century, 200 born in the seventeenth and 200 in the eighteenth. This error makes any comparison from century to century impossible as far as raw data are concerned, since the criterion of choice is arbitrarily variable from century to century. However, Pottinger made an inventory of 4,951 books written by the 600 authors and dated each work.

This inventory makes Pottinger's data comparable from century to century. Starting with his sample, one has only to tabulate (by decades) the number of authors producing, then the number of works written during each of those periods. By dividing the number of works produced by the number of authors, it is possible to establish a curve of productivity such as the one below:

Periods	Works / Authors	Periods	Works / Authors
1550-60	4.0	1680-90	2.7
1560-70	4.1	1690-1700	2.8
1570-80	3.6	1700-10	2.5
1580-90	2.9	1710-20	2.0
1590-1600	2.2	1720-30	1.7
1600-10	2.5	1730-40	2.0
1610-20	3.3	1740-50	2.0
1620-30	2.7	1750-60	2.7
1630-40	4.0	1760-70	2.7
1640-50	4.5	1770-80	2.4
1650-60	3.6	1780-90	3.6
1660-70	3.6	1790-1800	1.6
1670-80	3.4		

Now in my *Sociology of Literature*, I gave an "age curve" of writers based on a sampling of 937 writers from the sixteenth to the nineteenth century. This sample, also established by methods analogous to those used by Lehman, is quite different from Pottinger's. At each date on the chart, the age curve is formed by the percentage of writers less than forty years old who are now writing in relation to the total number of writers now producing. It has a characteristic shape which depends, as I have shown, on political events or, more exactly, on the succession of groups of writers having supremacy. For the period corresponding to the three centuries studied by Pottinger, here are my figures in periods of ten years:

Periods	%	Authors 40 Years / Total Authors	Periods	%	Authors 40 Years / Total Authors
1550-60	71.2		1680-90	30.0	
1560-70	67.6		1690-1700	29.1	
1570-80	45.0		1700-1710	28.1	
1580-90	29.9		1710-20	29.8	
1590-1600	34.3		1720-30	34.6	
1600-10	35.3		1730-40	39.6	
1610-20	44.2		1740-50	46.4	
1620-30	59.4		1750-1760	45.2	
1630-40	64.6		1760-70	42.2	
1640-50	54.7		1770-80	40.0	
1650-60	50.2		1780-90	48.1	
1660-70	45.4		1790-1800	54.6	
1670-80	38.2				

If we superimpose one curve on the other (the curve of productivity established according to Pottinger's figures and the aforementioned age curve), we can see that they coincide almost perfectly— *but with a lag of about twenty years.*

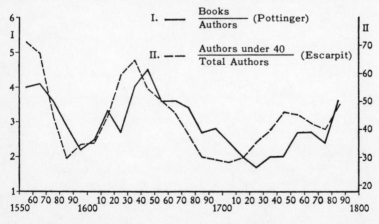

So we may suppose that the range of influence of the aging or the rejuvenation of the literary population on productivity is felt only after a delay of twenty years. Therefore, it is not immediately that a group of writers loses its supremacy and that a new group of writers in its twenties is born to literature, but twenty years later, when the leader of that new group reaches the age of forty.

Forty is not the beginning of sterility, but rather the point of equilibrium where the influences of two successive generations meet head on. Of course, we mean here generation in the widest sense of the word, including not only the team of producers of literature, but also the corresponding section of consumers. The significance of this age is neither biological nor psychological, but sociological. It is the average age when a writer finally acquires his social dimension.